Practical Behaviour Management Solutions for Children and Teens with **Autism**

of related interest

Fun with Messy Play
Ideas and Activities for Children with Special Needs
Tracey Beckerleg
ISBN 978 1 84310 641 8

Hints and Tips for Helping Children with Autism Spectrum Disorders
Useful Strategies for Home, School, and the Community
Dion E. Betts and Nancy J. Patrick
ISBN 978 1 84310 896 2

Helping Children with Complex Needs Bounce Back
Resilient Therapy™ for Parents and Professionals
Kim Aumann and Angie Hart
Illustrated by Chloe Gerhardt
ISBN 978 1 84310 948 8

First Steps in Intervention with Your Child with Autism
Frameworks for Communication
Phil Christie, Elizabeth Newson OBE, Wendy Prevezer and Susie Chandler
Illustrated by Pamela Venus
ISBN 978 1 84905 011 1

Group Interventions for Children with Autism Spectrum Disorders
A Focus on Social Competency and Social Skills
Albert J. Cotugno
ISBN 978 1 84310 910 5

Art as an Early Intervention Tool for Children with Autism
Nicole Martin
ISBN 978 1 84905 807 0

Practical Behaviour Management Solutions for Children and Teens with **Autism**

THE 5P APPROACH

LINDA MILLER

Jessica Kingsley Publishers
London and Philadelphia

First published in 2010
by Jessica Kingsley Publishers
116 Pentonville Road
London N1 9JB, UK
and
400 Market Street, Suite 400
Philadelphia, PA 19106, USA

www.jkp.com

Library of Congress Cataloging in Publication Data
Miller, Linda (Linda Janice)
    Practical behaviour management solutions for children and teens with autism : the 5P approach / Linda Miller.
        p. ; cm.
    Includes bibliographical references and index.
    ISBN 978-1-84905-038-8 (pb : alk. paper) 1. Autism in children. 2. Autism in adolescence. I. Title.
    [DNLM: 1. Autistic Disorder--therapy. 2. Adolescent. 3. Behavior Therapy--methods. 4. Child. WM 203.5 M648p 2009]
    RJ506.A9M585 2009
    618.92'85882--dc22

                                                        2009012318

British Library Cataloguing in Publication Data
A CIP catalogue record for this book is available from the British Library

ISBN 978 1 84905 038 8

Printed and bound in Great Britain by
Athenaeum Press, Gateshead, Tyne and Wear

I could not have written this book without all the help and support of the many teachers, parents, children and young people I have worked with throughout my career. I would particularly like to thank my husband Ian, whose encouragement and words of wisdom have been invaluable.

Contents

List of Tables

List of Figures

Central Insert

The 5P Intervention Framework Record

The 5P Approach Additional Materials (see Chapter 6)

* These materials are photocopiable.

Introduction

About this book

In my work with children and young people with autistic spectrum disorders, I am often asked by parents, teachers and other professionals for guidance and practical help in dealing with the difficult and challenging behaviours they meet on a daily basis. There are lots of places where you can find detailed information about common forms of behaviour problems which occur in autism, and what might be done to prevent or address them, but the reality is that teachers, parents and others are often simply overwhelmed by the sheer range and number of behaviour problems which confront them. Where do you start? And what happens when, in managing one set of problems, another gets worse – or a new problem appears? It is also very hard to find anything which helps with *individual* problems encountered and which approaches issues on the basis of *this* child, *this* place, *this* time, *this* context. Perhaps most importantly, there is little concrete information written in the context of behaviour management which provides guidance on preventing problems before they even arise. Facing all of these challenges can be very daunting, and it is with this in mind that the approach outlined in this book took shape.

The 5P Approach is a practical programme which can be used by professionals and parents who want a better understanding about the behaviour of children and young people with autistic spectrum disorders and how to prevent problems from arising, and who want help with the process of managing behaviour change. The framework is written within the context of conclusions drawn by professionals in the field of autism who suggest that behaviour issues only occur in situations where we have not created an autism-friendly environment or where we have failed to understand or adapt to issues which arise. Although primarily about managing behaviour, at its core is a focus on prevention rather than 'cure'. The 5P Approach therefore promotes establishing good foundations, or best autism practice, thus creating an environment where behaviour issues are at a minimum. It also recognizes, however, that realistically there will always be times where parents, teachers and other professionals encounter situations they find hard to handle (often on a daily basis) and that they look for support in dealing with them. With this in mind, the 5P Approach aims to provide a framework which helps to solve problems but also promotes long-term change and prevention.

The strategies and framework outlined in this book are designed specifically to take account of what we know about autistic spectrum disorders and the distinct way of thinking (the cognitive style) which characterizes them. Everything is then underpinned by learning theory, that is, what we know about how we learn.

What it aims to do

The book outlines a *framework* for behaviour intervention. Although there are some practical examples and useful tips, it does not simply provide a list of difficult behaviours and instructions on what could be done to change them (i.e. if he or she does this – then do this). Instead it sets out a clear pathway to follow, adopting right from the start a practical solution-focused problem-solving approach. The five-step pathway takes you from identifying behaviour and understanding the reason it occurs through to planning and implementing a comprehensive intervention programme. The approach therefore provides a clear process to follow, one step at a time, and a framework for collecting and using all the information needed for each stage. Each 'P' represents a stage or step in the process:

1 = **P**rofiling

2 = **P**rioritizing

3 = **P**roblem Analysis

4 = **P**roblem Solving

5 = **P**lanning.

The 5P Approach aims to provide a complete package which can be used time and time again, and which provides a solution whatever the circumstances. While clearly defining the steps you need to take, it also allows for flexibility in the range of materials provided which can be used according to need and individual situations. Within the overall framework there is an emphasis on promoting and encouraging the development of skills and independence of the children and young people involved in the programme. The aim of the approach is to look at behaviour as an integral part of the whole picture, not as isolated events. In this way, strategies can be developed to anticipate and head off problems before they arise. The framework adopts a model which builds on previous experience, with each new strategy devised then becoming part of the everyday 'toolkit'. Every problem encountered therefore teaches the adult more about the individual with autism. This leads to an incremental development and refinement of the autism-friendly environment and an approach tailor-made for each individual.

The strategies and approaches to behaviour intervention which this book brings together have been used in my work as an autism specialist educational psychologist. All of the materials have been tried and tested within schools and with parents, and have been designed specifically with teachers and parents in mind. The materials included in this book have been revised and modified taking account of the views of those using them in their everyday work.

What makes it different?

Several books in this field focus on suggesting strategies for managing and changing behaviour in children with autism. Some look at specific areas such as anger management, toilet training, etc., providing activities and recommending strategies to solve the problem. Others provide more general guidance on how to manage commonly occurring behaviour problems. The focus within this book however is on the 'how to do it' rather than the 'what to do', providing a framework and approach which can be applied to all aspects of behaviour change.

Using knowledge about autism and related disorders, and taking account of national recommendations in relation to intervention and teaching approaches which work best, the approach outlined in this book places behavioural change within the wider picture of overall intervention.

The approach brings together a number of elements which together form an overall strategy which is essential for successful behaviour management. These include:

- organizing an appropriate environment

- teaching new skills and coping strategies

- preventing and diverting behaviour

- dealing directly with behaviour difficulties.

Thus, the approach provides a 'whole picture' which has a clear focus on anticipating and preventing difficulties from arising rather than simply reacting to or coping with behaviours which have already occurred. The aim therefore is to reduce the number of times behaviour difficulties occur and to empower the adults involved by providing them with guidance for recognizing when a problem is likely to occur and a clear plan of what to do if a problem arises. As the approach places emphasis on identifying and preventing behaviour issues arising, there is also a focus on supporting the individual in developing independence and self-management.

Using a distinctive colour coding or 'traffic light' system, the 5P Approach provides clear visual reminders and a means of developing a common terminology and understanding amongst the adults (and the children and young people) involved and encourages consistency of approach. In addition to the guidance provided, the book contains numerous templates and visual representations which support the process and provide 'concrete' means of recording and representing the elements of the programme.

The 5P Approach has been widely used to plan programmes for individual children and young people with parents, teachers and professionals within whole class situations and even across whole schools.

How this book is set out

The book begins with an overview of what you need to know about autistic spectrum disorders in order to understand and effect behaviour change. It looks at the nature of autistic thinking and how this might affect behaviour, and discusses the commonly used recommendations for promoting good practice within the field of intervention.

This is followed by a general overview of the 5P Approach as set out within the book, identifying the five elements involved (Profiling, Prioritizing, Problem Analysis, Problem Solving and Planning) and explaining their importance to the process. The book then looks in detail at each of these, considering the practical aspects and materials which support each stage. For the final element, Planning (arguably the most important!), the book looks at how all the elements are brought together to plan a behaviour intervention programme. This also includes additional guidance which supports the Planning phase and concludes with the formation of the Intervention Framework. It is this which clearly sets out all the elements of the intervention plan which is then put into practical use.

The book then goes on to provide a step-by-step guide on how to 'make a start' and follow the 5P Approach from start to finish. This includes a checklist to aid the process, an Intervention Record pack and a template which is used to provide an 'at a glance' record of the Intervention Framework.

Further sections in the book provide additional guidance to support stages of the 5P process with materials for making observations, teaching new skills and using reward systems.

There are also some additional general strategies and ideas which will provide further resources for establishing best practice and help with 'staying Green'. This includes information on using the traffic light system with individuals and class groups and also looks specifically at how the 5P Approach and its materials can be used to support children and young people in managing their emotions. The final chapter provides examples of completed Intervention Frameworks for four case studies, to show how the 5P Approach works in practice.

How to use the book

The first thing to do is to read through to get an overview of the whole process and an understanding of all the elements involved. You can do this either as an individual parent or teacher, or as part of a group – family, professional or both. If you are working in a group, share ideas about how it can best be put into practice in your particular situation.

The next step is to use the guidance to aid your behaviour intervention planning. By following the step-by-step guide, you can work through the problem-solving process drawing on information and materials provided elsewhere in the book as needed. With your intervention plan in place, you are ready to put it into practice. Then, wherever you are in the process, the guide will be there to help you through any difficulties. If you persevere, and stick to the plan, you really can make a difference!

CHAPTER 1

Autism and Related Disorders – Understanding Behaviour

Before embarking on any work to prevent or manage behaviour, an understanding of the nature of autism and the implications this may have in relation to behaviour is essential. This first chapter explores the nature of autism and related disorders and begins with an overview of what you need to know about autistic spectrum disorders in order to understand and effect behaviour change. It looks at the nature of autism, examines what is meant by 'autistic thinking' and how this might affect behaviour, and looks at other related factors. It sets out to examine the nature of autism and related disorders, diagnosis and terminology, why children and young people with autism and related disorders sometimes behave differently (current theories about autistic thinking) and why behaviour difficulties might occur. The next chapter explores 'What can we do about it?' and looks at the importance of establishing 'foundations' and encouraging best practice as a means to prevent behaviour issues from arising.

Many books, papers and articles have been written which describe in detail the nature of autistic spectrum disorders, and there is now a wealth of information to be found on the web on all aspects of autism. Sites such as Research Autism (www.researchautism.net) and The National Autistic Society (www.nas.org.uk) are particularly informative.

National guidance publications can also be a good source of general information relating to autism. Two such publications are *Autistic Spectrum Disorders: Good Practice Guidance*, produced in 2002 by the then Department For Education and Skills, and the *National Autism Plan for Children* (known as NAP-C), produced from the work of the National Initiative: Autism Screening and Assessment (NIASA) – which drew together a core group of experts from a wide range of disciplines – and published by The National Autistic Society (NAS) in collaboration with the Royal College of Paediatrics and Child Health.

Publications by authors such as Lorna Wing, Judith Gould, Rita Jordan, Tony Attwood, Stuart Powell, Francesca Happe, Simon Baron Cohen and Patricia Howlin, to name a few, are all good sources of well-researched and up-to-date information covering a wide range of areas including identification, current theories and intervention practice. (See Further reading at the end of this chapter.)

This book, with its focus on behaviour intervention, does not therefore set out to provide in-depth information on autism as this can be found elsewhere in much greater detail. There is a need however to give an overview of the nature of autism and related disorders and to set out the information used to underpin the 5P Approach. We begin by looking at the issue of terminology.

An 'autistic spectrum'

The term 'autistic spectrum disorder' (ASD) is now commonly used as a generic term to describe individuals who have autism or autistic type features. The notion of a spectrum rather than one single disorder reflects the considerable differences between individuals with autism. The effects of autism can be mild or severe and can, in turn, be affected by environmental factors and any within-child factors such as additional disabilities. It is therefore the overall pattern of behaviour and difficulties which is considered rather than any one feature on its own. Autistic spectrum disorder is a popular term that defines the wide spectrum of related disorders including the classical form of the disorder as well as closely related disabilities that share many of the core characteristics. Recent use of the term 'autistic spectrum condition' (ASC) has emerged and is currently subject to debate.

Autistic spectrum disorders are characterized by core features known as the Triad of Impairments which are still used as the basis for diagnosis in both the UK (using the ICD-10) and the USA (using the DSM-

IV). The term ASD, although the most common term used nowadays, is still not recognized as a pure *diagnostic* term. Diagnostic terms included within autistic spectrum disorder are:

- autism (sometimes known as classic autism)

- Asperger syndrome

- pervasive developmental disorder – not otherwise specified (PDD–NOS)

- Rett syndrome

- childhood disintegrative disorder

- semantic pragmatic disorder.

How do we recognize autism? The Triad of Impairments

Autism is recognized through use of the Triad of Impairments – three core features which describe areas of difficulty found in all people with an autistic spectrum disorder, whatever the form. The three areas which form the Triad of Impairments are shown in Figure 1.1.

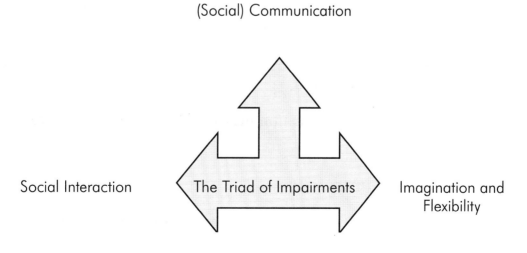

Figure 1.1 The Triad of Impairments

Although there is speculation that one day a diagnosis of autism may be made using biological or physical features, the Triad of Impairments originally identified by Lorna Wing and Judith Gould (1979) is still used as a basis for diagnosis of the disorder and is commonly accepted to represent the 'core' presenting features of ASD. All people diagnosed with autism share these three common features, although within each individual they may present in very different ways and to differing degrees.

Difficulty with social communication

Individuals with autistic spectrum disorder all have difficulties with some aspects of communication but these can vary considerably. Some may be non-verbal or have very limited speech, whereas others may have lots of expressive language but have problems with what are called 'higher order' language skills – the nuances of using language, such as interpretation of ambiguous language, making inferences and deductions, understanding jokes and sarcasm, etc. Main areas of difficulty included within this section therefore include:

- expressive and receptive language (speaking and understanding)

- expressing needs, feelings and views

- understanding and interpreting the communication of others (both verbal and non-verbal)

- the social rules of communication (turn taking, role as a communication partner, etc.)

- functional communication (using language to communicate).

Difficulty with social interaction

All individuals with autistic spectrum disorder have difficulties with some aspects of social interaction, but again these can take many forms. Some individuals may show a dislike or avoidance of interaction tending to be solitary and self-absorbed. Others may want and actively seek interaction with others but not know how to initiate or sustain relationships with others.

In summary, areas of difficulty with social interaction in ASD may include:

- understanding the rules of social interaction

- making and sustaining friendships

- interpreting and expressing own emotions and feelings

- interpreting others' intentions and understanding people

- understanding and predicting others' feelings and reactions.

Difficulty with imagination or flexibility

Problems in this area of the Triad of Impairments have sometimes been confused with a general lack of imagination. Now more commonly termed 'flexibility', difficulties relate to problems which arise from not being able to think flexibly or make connections.

To put it more generally, a lack of flexibility is commonly thought of as:

- rigidity in thinking and behaviour

- ritualistic behaviour

- difficulties with selectivity or narrow focus

- narrow interests and obsessions.

The reason that lack of flexibility is often thought of only in these terms is because these are the areas that are associated with behaviour difficulty and high anxiety. However, difficulty with flexibility in thinking also affects other behaviour, causing problems such as:

- poor generalization of skills, behaviours and knowledge (this of course affects the *functional* use of skills)

- difficulties with predicting and anticipating

- poor decision-making and problem-solving.

An individual with a diagnosis of autism or one of the related disorders will always present with difficulties in all three of the Triad areas, but the degree to which difficulties occur in each area may differ hugely. Therefore, each individual with autism will have an individual profile. This means that behaviour difficulties which occur as a result of underlying problems are also different for each individual. Although we can sometimes make generalizations in relation to behaviour prevention or behaviour management, issues relating to behaviour will need to be approached on the basis of *this* individual, *this* place, *this* time, *this* context.

Autistic thinking – what theories are used to explain autism?

Although individuals with autistic spectrum disorders share this common 'core' of features (the Triad of Impairments), they are often very different individuals. This, of course, has implications for behaviour problem solving and intervention planning and this is an issue that is addressed time and time again within this book.

In recent years researchers looking more closely at the nature and possible causes of autism have begun to look for precursors to the presenting Triad of Impairments (which are, after all, presenting *behaviours* which we observe). In this way they have been able to look more closely at the underlying factors which may be linked to causation.

Many researchers describe people with autistic spectrum disorder as having a distinct cognitive style. In other words, a different way of taking in, processing and interpreting information – a different way of thinking.

Current theories which add to our understanding of how this occurs and give real insight into the nature of autistic behaviour are Theory of Mind, Central Coherence, and Executive Function.

Theory of Mind

Theory of Mind is a 'Mental State' concept (a general condition within someone's mind) which can be used to explain how the characteristics of autistic spectrum disorders arise. People with ASD are said to have a deficit in Theory of Mind. The theory was launched in 1985 by Simon Baron-Cohen, Alan Leslie and Uta Frith in their article 'Does the autistic child have a theory of mind?'

The Theory of Mind hypothesis suggests that many individuals with ASD are not able to understand that other people have their own thoughts, beliefs, intentions and desires which both determine and effect their presenting behaviour. This difficulty also includes a lack of understanding that people vary in their thinking (i.e. they don't all think the same!) and that because they think differently they may also behave differently. Difficulty with Theory of Mind therefore also leads to problems in understanding other people's attitudes, beliefs and emotions or even in understanding that they have emotions. By not understanding that other people think differently from themselves, individuals with ASD have problems relating socially to others and in communicating with them. ASD individuals may not be able to anticipate what others will say or do in various situations and may also have difficulty in understanding that their friends or relatives have thoughts and emotions which differ from their own. This may well lead to them appearing to be self-centred, uncaring or odd. The implications arising from an absence of a Theory of Mind can therefore be linked to the behaviours detailed within the Triad of Impairments.

However, not all individuals with ASD have the same level of impairment in Theory of Mind and, as in other areas of the disorder, a continuum of skills in this area rather than absence or presence is a more appropriate description of the difficulties which occur (see Table 1.1).

Central Coherence

This theory was first proposed by Uta Frith in 1989. The theory suggests that the deficits of autism stem from a single cause at the cognitive level (thinking, information processing) which again, as in Theory of Mind, gives rise to a distinct autistic cognitive style. Central Coherence is characterized by difficulties with integrating information or putting information together to obtain an overall picture. People who do not have difficulty with this area and who have good Central Coherence

Table 1.1 Theory of Mind

Impaired Theory of Mind ⟶	Good Theory of Mind
Difficulty putting yourself in someone's shoes – seeing things from their point of view (empathy).	Understanding that other people have *their own* thoughts, beliefs, intentions and desires which are *different* from yours.
Difficulty understanding implied meanings. Poor use of social cues to help infer the meaning of words.	Recognizing that individuals may vary in their thoughts or beliefs and that these variations lead to differences in behaviour.
Difficulty understanding and predicting others' behaviour – difficulty inferring intention from action.	Predicting what a person thinks about another person's beliefs or thoughts and how others may interpret a situation.

demonstrate an ability to process information at a global level. That is they show a natural tendency to draw information together to construct a bigger, more context-related picture. Examples of Central Coherence include:

- getting the gist or forming an overall picture rather than looking at individual parts

- pulling together information for meaning as opposed to recalling individual elements

- processing information in context, taking account of all aspects and using this to add meaning.

Frith suggested that Central Coherence is disturbed or different in individuals with ASD and that this is characterized by a focus on parts rather than the whole (i.e. missing the whole picture). Individuals with poor Central Coherence should therefore be good at tasks which focus on local information (parts, attention to visual detail) rather than those which focus on global meaning (the whole picture).

Those with poor Central Coherence experience difficulties with, amongst other things:

- seeing the whole or bigger picture

- interpreting ambiguous language and absurdities

- taking account of context to aid understanding

- comprehension of stories

- inference and deduction

- making connections or semantic links

- seeing life as anything but a succession of isolated instances

- selectivity or narrow focus.

From the examples above, it is easy to see how difficulties with Central Coherence can be linked to some of the core features found within the Triad of Impairments.

Executive Function

The term Executive Function is used to describe higher level functions such as planning and organizing, using working memory, controlling impulses, etc. This also includes initiating and monitoring actions and is linked to mental flexibility. Executive Functions are said to influence the simpler or lower level functions such as attention and motor skills. Executive Functions are frequently said to be impaired in individuals with ASD, and there are also many links between difficulty in this aspect of processing and other neuro-developmental disorders such as attention deficit hyperactivity disorder (ADHD) and dyspraxia, which therefore have some presenting behaviours or problems in common with ASD.

Skills typically associated with Executive Function include:

- planning

- organizing

- sequencing

- self-monitoring

- controlling impulses

- controlling attention

- goal-directed behaviour.

The behaviour of individuals with poor Executive Function is often rigid and inflexible. They are frequently impulsive, having difficulty holding back a response. They may have a large store of knowledge but have trouble applying this knowledge meaningfully (thinking, planning and doing!). They often seem narrowly focused on detail and cannot see the whole picture (note links and similarities with Central Coherence).

Difficulties with Executive Function can therefore also be linked to some of the core features within the Triad of Impairments, particularly flexibility of thought, one of the core features of the Triad.

Understanding behaviour

All three of these theories add greatly to our understanding of autistic thinking and to how a different way of interpreting information may lead to differences in behaviour. They are particularly useful in explaining deficits in those individuals who have what is often termed 'higher functioning' autism as they give more detail to the behaviours listed within the Triad of Impairments or diagnostic criteria.

There are many examples of how having a different way of interpreting information may lead to the difficulties or differences associated with autism and which may, in turn, lead to problems with behaviour. For example, problems with social interaction may stem from difficulty understanding and predicting others' feelings and reactions or with interpreting others' intentions. These can be linked to poor Theory of Mind (difficulty in putting yourself in another's shoes) and poor Central Coherence (difficulty seeing the whole picture). Here is an example of what can happen; how would you interpret the picture in Figure 1.2? Crying? Sadness? Upset?

Figure 1.2 Central Coherence and emotions

In fact there are many possible differing interpretations, as shown in Figure 1.3.

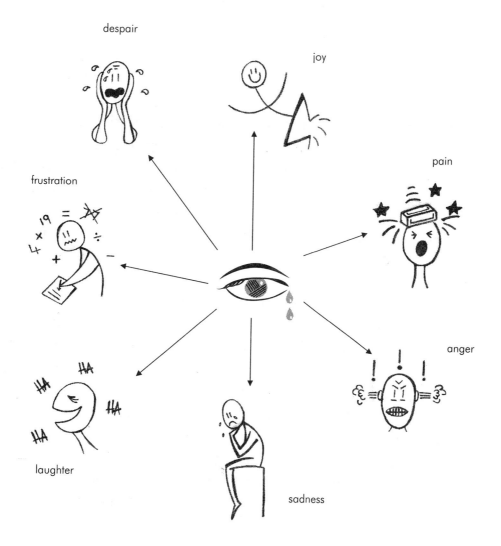

Figure 1.3 Central Coherence and emotions 2

But how do we decide which is which? We interpret situations using far more information than just a facial expression. We do this by:

- looking at body language

- listening to volume and tone of voice and the sounds made

- 'knowing' the situation or context

- observing others' reactions

- thinking back to past experiences

- seeing the whole picture!

Whenever we interpret situations, we need to see the whole picture to make sense of what we see and experience. What happens then when an individual fails to see the whole picture? What if you only focus on the tears? What if you only associate tears with sadness (because of a tendency for narrow focus, difficulty adapting to different situations, etc.)? What if in reality they are tears of laughter? Confusion? Frustration? Fear? Anger? It doesn't take much to put yourself in the shoes of the individual with ASD (something he or she couldn't do). Think about how you would behave in this situation. It is easy to see how behaviour difficulties are caused by underlying difficulties as described above.

It is important therefore when working with individuals with ASD to see any behaviour differences or difficulties in the context of the way the individual interprets situations and processes information. It is this understanding that forms the basis of prevention. Table 1.2 gives some other examples of how a different way of thinking might affect behaviour and lead to difficulty for the individual with ASD.

Examples such as this highlight the importance of understanding the individual, understanding the situation in which the behaviour is occurring and in using that information to plan for prevention. This is a crucial element of the 5P Approach which will emerge later in this book.

Sensory processing issues

In addition to the above theories, there has been much recent focus on sensory processing issues in people with ASD. Many adults with ASD have described differences in sensory processing and the anxieties and difficulties that can result. Increasingly, practitioners working with children and young people with autism are becoming aware of the important part sensory issues play in preventing access to learning and

Table 1.2 ASD cognitive style

Cognitive difficulties which may arise	Interpretation problems which may result
Difficulty putting yourself in someone's shoes – seeing things from their point of view (Theory of Mind).	Why did he hit me when I told him he was silly? Why won't she give me her best pencil? I didn't know she would cry. Why is he angry? I don't see why they can't play with me.
Difficulty adjusting behaviour according to demands of the immediate setting (Executive Function, Central Coherence).	Why is it wrong to call my teacher 'mate'? Why is it wrong to speak to strangers? Why should I sit quietly in assembly?
Difficulty controlling impulses (Executive Function).	I didn't mean to call out in class. I didn't stop to think. I just ran…
Difficulty understanding and predicting others' behaviour – difficulty inferring intention from action (Theory of Mind).	I thought he was going to be my friend. I thought she was going to hit me. I thought she was going to give me a present. I thought he would give me the ball.
Difficulty taking account of context to aid understanding (Central Coherence).	When she said find a 'pair', I couldn't see any fruit. She said 'pull your socks up' – I am wearing tights! Why is he cross? He said take this chair…
Difficulty estimating the passage of time, i.e. poor sense of time (Executive Function).	When will this finish? When can I go home? When can I have lunch? How long is this maths lesson? I am going to be here forever!

continued on next page

Table 1.2 ASD cognitive style *cont.*

Cognitive difficulties which may arise	Interpretation problems which may result
Difficulty carrying out tasks/behaviour in a staged, organized way, i.e. seeing a task through from beginning to end (Executive Function).	How do I get changed for PE? How do I plan this science experiment? What do I need to make a picture? How do I get to school on the bus?
Difficulty understanding implied meanings. Poor use of social cues to help infer the meaning of words (Theory of Mind).	Why are they all laughing? What is a joke? What is sarcasm? That doesn't make sense!
Selectivity or narrow focus (Central Coherence).	Why is talking about 'Star Wars' boring? I didn't know the teacher meant me when she spoke to the class. I didn't listen, I was watching the bird outside. There are so many things to choose from – I can't decide. It is *so* noisy – I can't shut the noise out.

social opportunities offered within the school setting and the extent to which sensory issues may affect behaviour and emotional well-being.

Earlier we looked at how difficulty with Central Coherence and Excutive Function may lead to problems with selectivity (so much information – you can't pick out the important part, i.e. overload) or narrow focus (seeking out the detail at the expense of the whole picture). In a similar way, sensory processing issues can lead to overload (hypersensitivity) or sensory-seeking (hyposensitivity) behaviour. Hyper- and hyposensitivity can relate to all the senses:

- vision
- hearing
- touch (tactility)
- taste

- smell

- proprioception (processing information about body position in space)

- vestibular system (processing movement, balance, etc.).

In simple terms, the process involves sensory information (from the body or environment) sent to the brain, which then organizes and processes the information and effects a response. Too much information processed causes hypersensitivity which then leads to sensory overload and avoidance. Too little information processed causes hyposensitivity which leads to sensory-seeking behaviour. Just as differences in cognitive style can be identified in people with ASD, differences in sensory processing can also occur. Difficulties and differences in sensory processing are, however, not confined to ASD and occur commonly in many individuals with wider processing problems. In any one individual the sensory profile may include some areas of hypersensitivity and some of hyposensitivity. If sensory issues appear to be present, it is therefore important to establish a clear picture through constructing a sensory profile.

The implications sensory issues may have in relation to behaviour are significant, and understanding an individual's sensory profile is an important element when planning an appropriate environment, when problem-solving behaviour issues which arise and when planning for intervention. Motor mannerisms and stereotyped behaviours are often linked to a diagnosis of autism and many of these may have a root in sensory processing. For example, flapping hands in front of eyes or staring intently at shiny objects or reflections may be an indication of hypo-vision.

It is easy to see how sensory issues may be a causal factor in any behaviour issues which may arise, particularly if they have not been recognized. For example, temper tantrums or high anxiety due to sensory overload, obsessive interest in movement (e.g. rocking) which prevents the child from accessing learning opportunities, and aversion to touch (leading to an 'aggressive' response when touched) are all common behaviours encountered within the school and home setting. With planning which takes account of these sensory needs, many of these issues can be avoided without the need for a detailed behaviour intervention programme. Assessment of an individual's sensory needs and provision of what is known as a 'sensory diet' is therefore an important element both in planning an appropriate environment and in planning behaviour change.

Having gained an overview of autism and how it presents, the next step is to use the information as a basis for building good foundations aimed at ensuring best practice in autism intervention and preventing issues from arising.

Further reading

Baron-Cohen, S. (1999) *Mindblindness: An Essay on Autism and Theory of Mind.* Cambridge, MA: MIT Press.

Bogdashina, O. (2003) *Sensory Perceptual Issues in Autism and Asperger Syndrome.* London: Jessica Kingsley Publishers.

Happe, F. (1994) *Autism: An Introduction to Psychological Theory.* London: UCL Press Ltd.

Howlin, P., Baron-Cohen, S. and Hadwin, J. (1999) *Teaching Children with Autism to Mind-Read.* Chichester: Wiley Press.

Jordan, R. (1999) *Autistic Spectrum Disorders: An Introductory Handbook for Practitioners.* London: David Fulton Publishers.

Powell, S. (2000) *Helping Children with Autism to Learn.* London: David Fulton Publishers.

Seach, D. (1998) *Autistic Spectrum Disorder – Positive Approaches for Teaching Children with ASD.* Tamworth: NASEN.

CHAPTER 2

In the Green Zone – Building the Foundations of Best Practice

Using and building on information from the last chapter, this chapter explores what we can do about preventing behaviour issues from arising, and looks at the importance of establishing 'foundations' and of encouraging best practice as a means of prevention.

The 5P Approach uses a unique and distinctive colour coding or traffic light system (Green, Amber and Red) to separate or distinguish differing strategies for planning intervention and managing behaviour, and links their use to the severity or type of behaviour occurring.

The first level is Green. The Green level represents where we want to be and where we want to stay: the 'foundations' of good practice where an autism-friendly environment generally prevents behaviour issues arising, where any difficult behaviour which does occur is managed through general everyday strategies, and where appropriate or desirable behaviour is rewarded using intrinsically motivating activities (good practice) or, where needed, through use of specific reward systems/strategies. The Green level therefore represents an autism-friendly environment, where behaviour issues are kept to a minimum and all adults have an autism 'toolkit' of strategies to use should any behaviour issues arise.

General or individual strategies?

There are many different views about how helpful it is to label a child's difficulties with terms such as autistic spectrum disorder. What is evident, however, is that some parents and teachers find it more helpful than others. Whatever the diagnosis or label, it is important to remember that every child is an individual and shows the autistic aspects of their behaviour uniquely. It is therefore vital to make sure that we know everything about that individual and use this information when planning and problem solving rather than relying solely on general principles. There are, however, general strategies and recommendations which address the common elements and features of ASD and it is these that form the basis of good practice (see below). These general principles, based on an understanding of the nature of autism and autistic thinking and the presentation of the Triad of Impairments, play a vitally important role in establishing good autism practice such as setting up an appropriate environment.

This book assumes, along with current thinking in the field, that if an appropriate autism-friendly or autism-specific environment is available, behaviour issues are far less likely to occur (Green level). However, it also recognizes that from time to time, however good the environment, behaviour issues will occur because:

- not all environments and experiences are autism-friendly

- not all individuals are alike

- people change

- circumstances change

- unexpected things happen!

When issues do arise, specific strategies may be needed and specific intervention planned. It is this that the major part of this book addresses. The 5P Approach, with its solution-focused emphasis, sets out to ensure that any strategies used quickly become part of the general approach (the autism-friendly environment) and are established as part of the foundations (getting back to Green!). This can be shown in the form of an intervention triangle (Figure 2.1) with the proportion of the triangle representing the amount of focus placed at each level. It shows

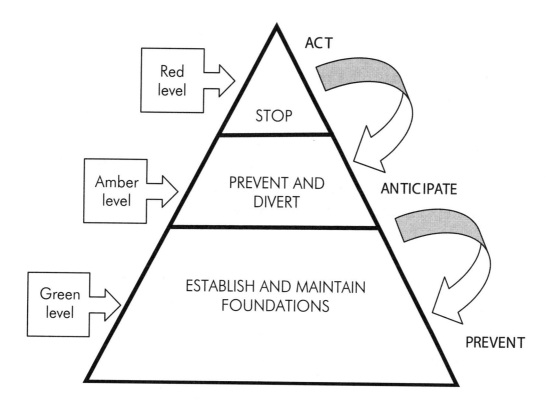

Figure 2.1 The 5P intervention triangle

a clear pathway from Red (the most difficult behaviour) back to Green as soon as possible. This move through traffic light colours and back to Green is a core theme of the 5P Approach.

General strategies for getting the environment right

The 5P Approach advocates the use of best practice in setting up an appropriate autism-friendly environment and sees this as playing the major role in preventing behaviour issues from arising and in meeting the needs of the individual with autistic spectrum disorder. Experts in the field of autism, such as Rita Jordan and Stuart Powell (1995, 1997), advocate the use of an autism-friendly environment which acknowledges that the way the learning and social environment is structured and organized and the teaching approaches used may contribute to the difficulties in communication and behaviour we observe. Creating and providing an environment which is specifically designed with autism in mind provides maximum opportunity for the individual with ASD to develop independence in their learning and communication, and socially. This view has since been developed further with national recommendations to create autism-friendly environments and autism-friendly schools. National guidance such as *Autistic Spectrum Disorders, Good Practice Guidance* (DfES 2002) and the *National Autism Plan for Children (NAP-C)* (NIASA 2002) also advocate the use of autism-friendly environments and strategies which take account of the distinct autistic style of thinking and interpreting information.

Establishing good foundations – the Green Zone!

The 5P Green Zone provides good foundations promoting best practice in autism with a view that, once these are in place, the frequency of any behaviour issues will be greatly reduced. Taking account of the distinct ASD cognitive style and learning preferences and including research-based best practice, the Green Zone or foundations should always include the following:

1. establishing the environment

2. establishing good communication systems

3. an ASD-specific approach to teaching and learning

4. use of ASD-specific strategies and interventions

5. individualization.

Establishing the environment

The ASD-specific environment takes account of:

- organization and structure

- sensory issues (adaptations of the environment, provision of a sensory diet).

Establishing good communication systems

This is done by creating a Total Communication Environment (for listening, understanding, expressing) with the use of:

- visual materials

- signs

- interactive approaches, etc.

Effective communication systems are two-way and best practice will ensure that communication is addressed from the point of view of both speaker and listener. It is essential to create a communication-rich environment which offers opportunity for communication of all types and actively encourages interaction in all aspects of the learning and social environment.

An ASD-specific approach to teaching and learning

An ASD-specific approach to teaching and learning offers an approach and curriculum in which:

- activities are functional, concrete and meaningful

- activities are intrinsically motivating (working with the ASD learning style)

- there is a focus on developing communication and interaction skills in the widest sense

- there is a focus on developing flexibility in thought and independence

- activities are used which integrate/embed sensory and communication targets and strategies into everyday functional tasks

- opportunities for regular sensory/learning breaks are built into the daily routine

- individual learning styles are catered for by using rule-based, play-based or sensory-based approaches.

Use of ASD-specific strategies and interventions

Research indicates that the use of an eclectic approach is likely to be the most successful form of intervention, particularly when specific strategies are tailored to meet individual needs. Specific strategies include approaches such as:

- TEACCH (Treatment and Education of Autistic and related Communication-handicapped CHildren)

- PECS (Picture Exchange Communication System)

- Intensive Interaction

- Non-directive communication therapy

- Social Stories

- Applied Behaviour Analysis.

Individualization

Good foundations allow for approaches and strategies to be tailored to meet individual needs. This would include:

- detailed profiling of the individual (know and understand that person)

- interpreting the above in line with what we know about the needs of the individual involved

- adapting approaches in line with what we know about the needs of the individual involved

- adding new strategies in line with proven success or new knowledge (learning from experience).

In common with expert thinking in the field, the 5P Approach takes the view that using best practice in autism will prevent many behaviour issues from arising. Therefore, before embarking on any complex programme to resolve behaviour issues, the first thing to do is to check the foundations (Green level). Making adjustments to the elements within the foundations may be all that is needed to prevent further behaviour issues arising, and there may be no need for a more complex behaviour intervention plan. The 5P Approach uses a simple foundations check as an aide-memoire – this is set out in Table 2.1.

Table 2.1 The 5P foundations check

Area	Things to look for
1. Establishing the environment (a) Organization and structure	Rooms organized and clutter free: • clear floor space • careful planning of furniture • systematic storage of materials and resources.
(b) Sensory issues	Organization and planning at all levels takes account of sensitivities and distractions relating to: • noise • olfactory issues • proprioception (i.e. physical proximity, hard/soft touch, etc.) • touch • visual (see above) • vestibular issues. Sensory diets/activities provided.
2. Establishing good communication systems	Adults adopt a communication style appropriate to the level and preferred communication style of the individual. Use of visual materials, signs, verbal communication as appropriate. Use of standardized visual materials (e.g. symbols and photos) throughout the environment appropriate to individual's level of understanding. Adults regard the individual with ASD as an active communication partner at all times. Adults take account of and listen to the voice of the individual.

continued on next page

Table 2.1 The 5P foundations check *cont.*

Area	*Things to look for*
3. An ASD-specific approach to teaching and learning	Activities are functional, concrete and meaningful.
	Activities are intrinsically motivating (working with the ASD learning style).
	There is a focus on developing communication and interaction skills in the widest sense.
	There is a focus on developing flexibility in thought and independence.
	Activities which integrate/embed sensory and communication targets and strategies into everyday functional tasks.
	Opportunities for regular sensory/learning breaks built into the daily routine.
	Approach suits/adapts to individual learning styles.
4. Use of ASD-specific strategies and interventions	Use of approaches such as TEACCH, PECS, Intensive Interaction, Non-directive communication therapy, etc.
	Do these link to learning style and preferences? i.e. Rule-based, play-based, sensory-based. (See 5P Profile for guidance.)
5. Individualization	Detailed profiling of the individual – know and understand that person. (See 5P Profile.)
	Interpretation of above in line with what is known about the needs of the individual involved.
	Approaches adapted in line with what is known about the needs of the individual involved.
	New strategies added in line with proven success or new knowledge (learning from experience).

Using your knowledge and profile of the child/young person, look carefully at each element of the foundations and consider the following:

- Does something need re-establishing?

- Does something need changing?

- Does something need adding, reducing or removing?

CHAPTER 3

Introducing the 5P Approach

Overview

The 5P Approach moves through a carefully defined process to ensure that behaviour issues are seen as part of a wider context and that all necessary areas are covered within the framework. It sets out a structured approach to intervention planning which uses five distinct stages, all of which contribute to the overall plan and are interdependent. To give an overview of the whole process, a brief summary of the five basic stages is recorded below.

1. Completing the 5P Profile

Based on the need to know the individual before any *specific* strategies can be developed, the first stage in the 5P Approach is to complete a profile (or 'pen portrait') of the child or young person. Not intended as an in-depth assessment, the Profile is used to give an overview and to highlight key information which will be used at different stages of the 5P Approach. Details of how to complete the Profile are included in the section on 'Creating a Profile' later in this chapter.

2. Identifying intervention Priorities

The second stage of the process is to begin to prioritize areas or behaviours identified as needing intervention. The 5P Approach uses a traffic light system to aid the prioritization process and also provides guidance as an aid to decision making. Further details of how to complete the prioritizing process and additional guidance are set out in the section on 'Prioritizing'.

3. Completing the Problem Analysis process

The third stage, Problem Analysis, signals the beginning of the problem-solving process and is one of the most important steps in the 5P Approach. This is primarily a process of information gathering. The 5P Approach uses an A BBB C chart (which differs from the commonly used ABC chart), observation and discussion to aid the information-gathering process. Details of how to complete the problem analysis process and additional guidance and materials can be found in the section on 'Problem Analysis'.

4. Completing the Problem Solving process

The fourth stage, Problem Solving, looks at *why* the identified behaviour occurs. During the problem-solving stage, the likely purpose or function of the behaviour is identified. Building upon information gained from the Profile and Problem Analysis stages, the next step is to construct a hypothesis or working theory to explain the reason the behaviour occurs. The 5P Approach uses a Problem Solving Flowchart to work systematically through the possible reasons why the behaviour might be occurring. This can then be used to form a hypothesis which is noted on the Problem Solving Summary Sheet. Details of how to complete the Problem Solving process, additional guidance and materials are included in the section on 'Problem Solving'.

5. Completing the Planning process

The final stage of the 5P Approach is the Planning stage. This is the most complex stage of the 5P Approach and draws together and makes use of information gained from all the previous stages. The 5P Approach uses a range of materials to aid the Planning process, including a flowchart which helps to identify which intervention strategies should be used. Tailor-made photocopiable materials for the Planning process include the Planning Flowchart, the Intervention Framework and the Intervention Hierarchy.

In addition to specific behaviour intervention strategies and guidance, the overall intervention plan brings together a number of other elements crucial to the success of the intervention, such as the teaching of new skills and the use of reward systems. An overall Intervention Framework is therefore constructed which brings together all of the elements identified within the Planning phase and provides a clear and whole picture of the overall plan. This Intervention Framework is recorded on the Intervention Framework Flowchart, which provides a concise visual representation of the overall plan. This can be photocopied and shared with all concerned in the intervention process. Details of how to complete the Planning process, additional guidance and materials are included in Chapter 4, 'Planning for Intervention'.

Photocopiable templates of all the essential materials are included in the Invervention Framework Record pack at the end of Chapter 4 (pp.83–97).

Stage 1 – Creating a Profile

Creating a 5P Profile is the first stage of the 5P Approach and places an emphasis on the need to 'know' the child or young person before embarking on any action to understand or change behaviour. Although all people with a diagnosis of autism may share the same common features (the Triad of Impairments) each person is very different and it is therefore important to know as much about the individual as possible before setting out any intervention or support. If you are taking account of best practice, have established good ASD foundations, and behaviour difficulties are still occurring, general strategies may not be enough. Specific strategies or programmes require more knowledge about the individual.

The use of the 5P Profile provides a visual 'pen portrait' of the child or young person with ASD. Not intended as an in-depth assessment, the Profile is used to highlight key information used within the 5P Approach. The Profile has six sections:

1. Likes and interests

2. Dislikes, fears and worries

3. Communication

4. Learning/cognitive style, strengths and preferences

5. Difficulties and weaknesses

6. Sensory issues.

An overview of the Profile is set out in Figure 3.1. A blank, photocopiable Profile can be found within the Intervention Framework Record pack (p.85). Information from each area is used within different stages of the 5P Approach. For example, information from sections 2, 3 and 5 helps to identify possible causes/purposes of the behaviour challenges which arise. Information from section 4 can help to pinpoint which strategies, methods and resources are likely to be successful in teaching the child or young person with ASD (the foundations) and also within the behaviour intervention process. Information from section 1 can be used at the 5P Planning stage to inform strategies which can be used for diversion, motivation and reward. Many children and young people with ASD have sensory preferences and sensory sensitivities. These are recorded within section 6 of the Profile. Information relating to the sensory side can be used in two ways: to inform the strategies used for diversion, breaks and reward, and also as part of the Problem Solving process.

Information from the Profile can also be used when establishing foundations for best practice. The information within the Profile can be used to ensure that all aspects have been taken into account when planning the environment and approaches to be used with the individual. It can also be used as a quick check to ensure sensory needs are being addressed and communication systems are in place, etc.

Once you have completed the Profile (and checked your foundations!) move on to Stage 2 – Prioritizing.

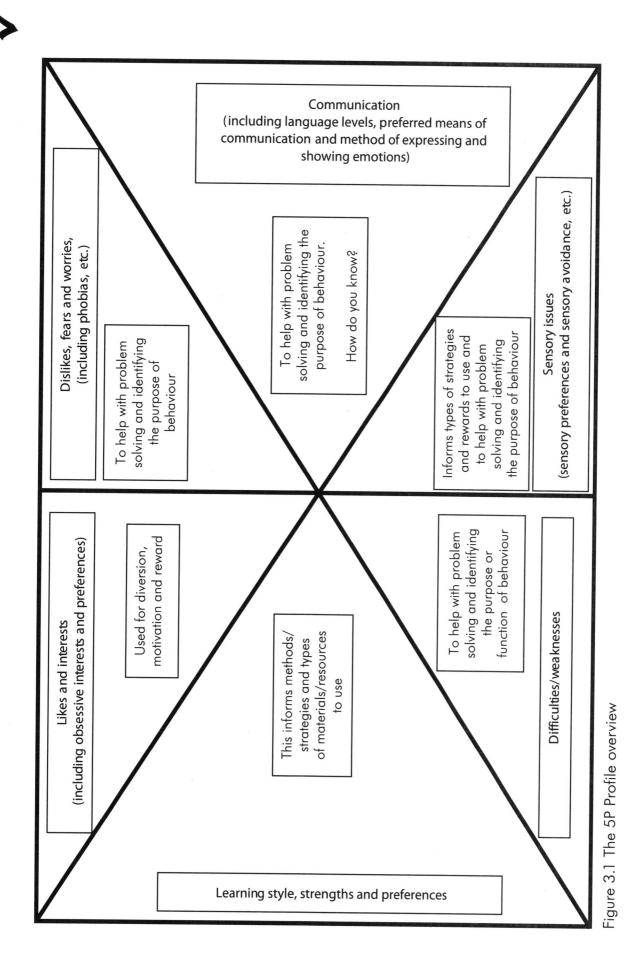

Figure 3.1 The 5P Profile overview

Stage 2 – Prioritizing

This section looks at the issue of prioritizing. We start from the position that, however well prepared, sometimes we can reach a stage where children and young people with ASD present us with so many behaviour challenges (or where we identify so many behaviours for change or intervention) that it can be difficult to know where to start. This is particularly relevant when a crisis point has been reached or at the beginning of a new placement or phase in the individual's school or home life.

Before we start, however, it is important to define what we mean by behaviour 'challenges'. The 5P Approach sees all behaviour as 'actions' (or lack of action or inactions). Behaviour which challenges is therefore not necessarily aggressive or difficult behaviour which causes harm to others or to the child or young person. Challenging behaviour may be any action or inaction which challenges access to learning or social opportunities. The 'Why change behaviour?' checklist in Table 3.1 prompts the beginning of a prioritizing process by providing a series of questions to aid decision making.

The 5P Approach uses a process of prioritizing behaviours into three categories according to the degree of severity/urgency (see Figure 3.2) and also provides an opportunity to re-think: 'does this behaviour *really* need to change?' The three categories are:

Green 1 priority represents 'I can live with this' – a situation where no specific action/strategies are needed other than best autism practice. Please note however that Green also includes behaviours identified to be increased or developed. This is used later in the Planning stage of the 5P Approach and is identified as Green 2.

Amber priority represents 'This needs addressing but can wait' – a situation where no specific action is needed at this stage or where the behaviour can be diverted rather than needing immediate and specific action (this could be a 'bubbling' behaviour which acts as a signal or precursor to a more difficult 'Red' behaviour).

Red priority represents a top priority where immediate action is needed.

Table 3.1 'Why change behaviour?' checklist

Questions to ask when prioritizing	Yes or no?
Is this behaviour a danger to X or others?	
Does this behaviour result in something/someone being harmed?	
Is this behaviour having a negative impact on others?	
Is this behaviour upsetting family life?	
Is this behaviour preventing something from happening? (e.g. teaching/progress)	
Does this behaviour break the rules (society/school/home, etc.)?	
Is this behaviour difficult to understand? (What is it communicating?)	
Is there is a better/more effective way of communicating than this?	

Notes:

_____

_____

_____

_____

_____

_____

_____

_____

_____

_____

_____

_____

_____

_____

_____

_____

_____

_____

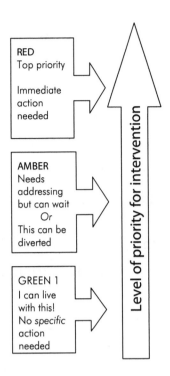

Figure 3.2 Prioritizing

You may already be able to identify your top priority for intervention and those behaviours you might divert but, if not, the first step in the prioritizing process is literally to write down all the areas identified for behaviour intervention (however trivial). These can be written as a list or, to make this a simpler, practical task (particularly good when prioritizing in a pair or group), by writing each behaviour on a small Post-it note. Once the list is complete, the process of prioritizing begins.

Taking each identified behaviour in turn, ask the Green, Amber and Red questions below and use the 'Why change behaviour?' checklist set out in Table 3.1 to help in the decision-making process.

Green 1 – Can you live with this behaviour without changing? (Will letting this go cause problems/prevent anything from happening?)

Amber – Can this wait or can this be diverted?

Red – Does this behaviour need tackling immediately?

If you are using Post-it notes it is easy to sort to Green, Amber and Red priorities and then re-sort within the Red category to get a hierarchy of urgency. This exercise of prioritizing, as well as pinpointing where to start, also provides opportunities for discussion amongst those working with the individual about how their priorities differ from others' and why this might be. Coming to an agreed priority list is really useful when planning intervention and it promotes teamwork.

Stage 3 – Problem Analysis

Now that you have prioritized and chosen the behaviour(s) which will be the focus for change, the next step is Problem Analysis. The Problem Analysis stage is really the first stage in the intervention problem-solving process, and one of the most important steps. Before finding a solution to the problem (by planning intervention), it is essential to have a clear picture of what is happening. When dealing with difficult and sometimes challenging behaviour, it is often hard to tease out the steps that lead up to the behaviour occurring or to recognize the consequences which that behaviour evokes. The use of an ABC chart (now used commonly within behaviour management programmes) provides a step-by-step guide in which to analyse what happens when a behaviour occurs. In the ABC chart, A stands for Antecedent, B for Behaviour and C for Consequence. The 5P Approach takes this one step further and introduces the use of an A BBB C chart which provides even more detail and a higher level of analysis.

'Trigger' or function?

When analysing behaviour, we are commonly encouraged to look for the 'trigger' or the particular action or event which occurs immediately before the behaviour occurs and which can thus be linked to its 'cause' (as the behaviour is thought to be occurring in response to this action or event). Sometimes this is easy to see, for example, hitting and shouting behaviour may be immediately preceded by a request to shut down the computer. At other times, when the trigger is not obvious, it is more helpful to consider what the *function* of the behaviour might be.

In this case no one event or action acts as a trigger as the behaviour may, for example, be the result of a build-up of stress, anxiety or anger. This type of behaviour can often, but not always, be linked to sensory needs or sensory aversion. For example, a child may become regularly angry or upset (the behaviour response) during a supermarket trip, so much so that he or she has to leave the shop (the consequence). When the behaviour occurs, the child has been in the supermarket for some time and no particular trigger can be identified, as nothing particular happens immediately before the upset. The function of the behaviour might be to reduce a sensory overload and avoid the noisy, bustling and bright atmosphere of the supermarket. This sensory overload may have built up over time rather than be a response to a specific event. Another example of a behaviour having a function rather than trigger would be the emergence of rocking or increased movement which serves to address a sensory need.

The A BBB C chart, specifically designed for the 5P Approach, is a useful tool to record precisely what happens when a particular behaviour occurs, and should be completed with information gained from the Profile in mind (i.e. likes, dislikes, sensory needs, etc.). Remember that at this point we are not problem *solving,* but an awareness of the possible function aids the recording of precise information (e.g. recording the environmental factors such as noise, light levels, etc.). This will provide all the information needed for the next stage in the 5P process. Before looking in detail at the A BBB C stages, it is best to begin by giving a clear description or definition of the behaviour. The 'Describing behaviour' chart in Table 3.2 can be used as a guide when summarizing the overall description of the behaviour you are analysing within the A BBB C chart.

Using the A BBB C chart

A – THE ANTECEDENT

This section deals with the lead up to the behaviour you are wishing to analyse. It is often easier to work through a series of questions to help focus thoughts on precise details. Useful questions for this section are:

Table 3.2 Describing behaviour

An active or physical response	A negative interaction		A self-stimulatory or sensory-based behaviour	An emotional response
	To Self	To Other		
Running away	Head banging	Hitting	Hand flapping	Crying
Climbing	Pinching	Biting	Rocking	Screaming
Throwing	Biting self	Kicking	Noise	Noise
Damaging/destructive	Hitting self, etc.	Spitting	Singing/humming	Facial expression
Dropping to floor	Other:	Punching, etc.	Flicking fingers	Verbal
Refusal to move		Other:	Flicking paper etc.	Anger/tantrum
Refusal to comply			Twiddling objects, etc.	Fear
Taking or grabbing			Other:	Frustration
Stamping feet, etc.				Enjoyment, etc.
Other:				Other:

- What happens before the behaviour occurs?

- When does it happen? (a particular time of day or during a particular activity)

- Where does it happen? (environmental issues)

- What do you think provokes it?

- Who is involved? (is a particular child or adult present when the behaviour occurs?)

BBB – THE BEHAVIOUR SEQUENCE

This section requires a detailed description of *exactly* what behaviour occurs, breaking this down into as much detail as possible. This is particularly important if the behaviour you are describing has more than one phase, for example, a facial expression, then a cry, then dropping to the floor, then kicking, etc. The BBB section of this chart provides a framework to break down the behaviour pattern into stages, from first signals and indicators through increasing problems or 'bubbling' behaviour to the most severe behaviour. Identifying the behaviours which occur at each of these stages is vital when planning for intervention. As the 5P Approach to intervention works on a staged method which uses different strategies according to the type and intensity of the behaviour which occurs, it is necessary to record the behaviour in a detailed and staged manner. The use of the A BBB C chart allows for the three stages of behaviour to be recorded:

B 1 – first signals or early indicators

B 2 – increasing problem indicators or emerging behaviours

B 3 – final stage behaviours – the most severe.

When completing this A BBB C chart for the first time, you may find that you do not have enough information to fully complete the detail required and that there is a need to go back and observe more closely or discuss issues further. Sometimes it may be useful to have a detailed or structured observation which can provide numerical information to support the monitoring of progress and effectiveness of the intervention.

This is particularly useful when addressing entrenched or self-injurious behaviour which needs more careful monitoring and a more detailed analysis.

Observations can focus on the length of time a behaviour occurs (the duration), the number of times a behaviour occurs (the frequency), or the presence or absence of a behaviour within a given time frame (interval sampling). Examples of observation recording can be found in Chapter 5, 'Additional Guidance and Supporting Materials', along with an example of a discussion record and prompt questions for discussion.

C – THE CONSEQUENCE (OR OUTCOME)

This section requires a detailed consideration of what the consequences of the behaviour are (i.e. what results from or happens after the targeted behaviour has occurred). Useful questions to ask at this stage are:

- What happens next? (immediately after the behaviour occurs)

- What do *you* do?

- What are the results for the child/young person? (e.g. getting something, avoiding something)

This last section of the chart is particularly important as it provides information which helps the problem-solving process (i.e. identifying the *reason* the behaviour occurs or its *function*).

An example of the A BBB C chart is set out in Table 3.3 and a blank chart is included within the Intervention Framework Record pack (p.87).

When Problem Analysis is complete, a summary from this stage is added to the Problem Solving Summary sheet (see 'Problem Solving' below).

Stage 4 – Problem Solving

Having obtained a clear picture of what happens when the targeted behaviour occurs, through the Problem Analysis stage, the next step is to look at *why* the behaviour occurs. During the Problem Solving

Table 3.3 The A BBB C chart example

Note: Does this occur as a single incident? or Is this a prolonged reaction?

Does the behaviour consist of a sequence of different behaviours/reactions? e.g. facial expression to vocalization to movement to aggression

Overall description of behaviour:

Antecedent	Behaviour			Consequence
A	**B**	**B**	**B**	**C**
What happens before? When? (time of day, particular activity?) Where does it happen? What provokes it? Who? (particular child/adult?)	What are the first signals? (early indications)	What are the first/emerging *behaviours*? (increasing problem indicators or 'bubbling' behaviour)	**Final stage** Behaviours (the most severe)	What happens next? What do *you* do? What are the results for the child/young person? (e.g. get something, avoid something, etc.)
	NB. Exactly what *behaviour* occurs? How often? How long does it last?			

stage, the likely purpose or function of the behaviour is identified. Information gained from the Profile and Problem Analysis stages is then used to construct a theory or hypothesis to explain the reason the behaviour occurs.

Frequently we find ourselves in the position of having to interpret the behaviour of a child or young person who may have difficulties in communicating their thoughts and feelings and who may, because of their distinct cognitive style, interpret and react to situations or information in a way that is different from that we might expect. For example, a child with a sensitivity to noise may react in response to a noisy, busy classroom; a child with rigid, inflexible behaviour and a preference for routine may react aggressively when presented with change or surprise (however pleasant the change or surprise may be). There is often a need therefore to put ourselves in the shoes of the individual with ASD and try to interpret why the behaviour is occurring. The 5P Approach uses a Problem Solving Flowchart to provide a basic functional assessment of a behaviour, which works systematically through the possible reasons why the behaviour might be occurring. The process involves asking a series of questions to narrow down the possible options, finally pointing to possible situations or reasons for the behaviour. This can then be used to form a hypothesis detailing the reason the behaviour is occurring. The hypothesis is recorded on the Problem Solving Summary sheet.

Caution! Identifying the function of a behaviour is a vital step in the behaviour intervention process but understanding why a behaviour occurs should not then lead us to accept or excuse a behaviour which has been considered to be undesirable or 'inappropriate' (re-visit the 'Why change behaviour?' guidance, Table 3.1). For example, a child may spit, hurt or verbally abuse as an expression of emotion which stems from a situation they find hard to understand. A child may scratch and bite as an expression of extreme anxiety or fear. Understanding the 'why' will lead us to consider how to prevent or pre-empt this from occurring but, once an undesirable or inappropriate behaviour has occurred, agreed actions and behaviour management strategies should be put into place (see Chapter 4).

From experience, it is often easy to accept a physical reaction from a young child (e.g. hitting) with the understanding that this is a reaction and has no aggressive intent, but accepting this without intervention or prevention has negative consequences. Children tend to get bigger and stronger and what was easy to deal with as a mild 'slap' may become much more difficult (and painful) to control as the child becomes a young adult. In addition, children and young people with autism have difficulty with communication and expression of emotions. Expression of an emotion by a physical reaction like this may be able to be interpreted by those who are caring for and teaching the individual with ASD, but simply accepting that this is a means of communication without change does not prepare the individual for the less accepting social world (by teaching the 'rules'), neither does it empower them by providing an alternative and more acceptable and effective means of communication. Similarly, accepting this behaviour as the 'norm' does not lead the individual with ASD to develop an understanding of the implications or the effect their behaviour has on others or to develop an understanding of others' emotions (Theory of Mind). The 5P Approach sets out a behaviour intervention strategy which aims to 'signal' when an undesirable or 'Red' behaviour occurs and provide an alternative means of communicating. It is important to state right from the start, however, that the 5P Approach *does not* advocate that punishment or sanction should be used to respond to undesirable behaviour but *does* advocate that a clear signal is used to communicate that a Red behaviour has occurred. Red strategies are explained in detail in Chapter 4.

Problem Solving step by step

Working out the function of a behaviour (the reason it occurs) relies greatly on the detail and quality of the information collected in the earlier stages. Some approaches to behaviour intervention or behaviour management begin with detailed functional analysis questionnaires which examine all aspects of the child's functioning, strengths, weaknesses, preferences and dislikes. These, although very useful, are time-consuming to complete. The 5P Approach uses in the first instance the quick reference flowchart as a means of functional assessment, using information gained from the earlier stages of the approach.

There are times of course where the function of the behaviour is still uncertain or the behaviour interventions put in place to date have been unsuccessful, and when a higher level of detail in the form of a structured, more detailed, functional assessment may be required. The 5P Approach suggests however that moving to this level of detail in the first instance may well be unnecessary, and the use of the materials here coupled with knowledge and understanding of the child is generally sufficient in order to form a correct hypothesis about why the behaviour occurs. The 5P Approach therefore sets out a staged problem-solving pathway as follows.

STEP 1

Using the Problem Solving Flowchart (p.88), work methodically through the questions, highlighting any items which may apply. This provides a visual summary outlining the possible function of the behaviour.

STEP 2

Construct a hypothesis which describes the purpose of the behaviour, using all the information taken from the chart, for example:

Behaviour = An expression of anger because child X is avoiding physical contact from others (dislikes children touching him/getting too close).

or

Behaviour = A means of communication to request a break when things get too much (too noisy – sensory overload).

STEP 3

Detail your hypothesis on the Problem Solving Summary sheet (p.89). (If information from the Problem Analysis stage has not already been added, do so now.)

Once this has been completed, move to the final stage – Planning.

CHAPTER 4

Planning for Intervention

Planning intervention is the last and the most complex stage of the 5P Approach and makes use of the information gained from all the previous stages.

Even if you have clearly identified the behaviour and the reason it occurs, choosing an appropriate strategy, planning action and ensuring consistency of approach are all difficult tasks. To make this simpler, the 5P Approach uses a Planning Flowchart to identify which intervention strategies would be the best to use for a particular problem. As with the Problem Solving Flowchart, the process involves asking a series of questions to narrow down the options, finally pinpointing approaches to be used within the overall Intervention Framework.

The term Intervention Framework is used to reflect the need to do more than simply construct a behaviour programme. To make things clearer, the same traffic light colour system is used to identify elements of the framework at different levels. Depending on the type of behaviour and reason it occurs, intervention planning often involves a complex mix of elements and more than simply immediate actions, for example, teaching new skills (also linked to rewards and motivators), teaching coping strategies and managing behaviour at Amber and Red levels. There are often therefore several elements within the planning process, as shown in Figure 4.1.

Given the complex nature of the Planning stage, it is easier to see this as a series of steps. An overview of the steps is set out below and a more detailed breakdown of each step follows.

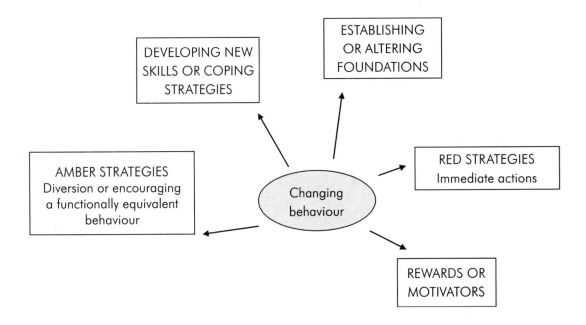

Figure 4.1 Planning overview

Planning step by step – an overview of the process

Step 1 – Identifying the elements of the Intervention Framework using the Planning Flowchart (p.90).

Step 2 – Starting to Plan using the Intervention Hierarchy (p.92). Things to consider:

- What foundations may need to change? (Green 1 level)

- What new skills will need to be taught?

- What reward system or reinforcing activities can be used (if appropriate or needed)?

- Which functionally equivalent behaviours (FEB) or diversion activities could be used (if necessary)? (Amber level)

- What actions or strategies might be needed? (Red level)

Record these on the Planning Summary sheet (p.91) for quick reference.

Note: Additional guidance is provided in Chapter 5 in relation to the teaching of new skills and the use of rewards and motivators.

Step 3 – Combining all the elements by constructing the overall Intervention Framework.

Step 1 – Using the Planning Flowchart

The Planning Flowchart is used to identify the elements needed within an Intervention Framework. Begin by working through the chart considering each question in turn and identify any elements which apply to this particular situation. At this stage it is easiest just to identify and mark which elements apply, returning to discuss and complete the detail once all the elements are identified. When answering the questions, information gained from the previous stages can be used to help inform decisions, for example, decisions on whether to divert or replace with a functionally equivalent behaviour are made taking account of the identified purpose or function of the behaviour from the Problem Solving stage. Diversion strategies can be identified using information from the Profile on a child/young person's likes and preferences, etc.

The first question 'Can this behaviour be changed by adjusting the foundations?' is a crucial one and may negate the need to move any further in constructing an Intervention Framework. In the longer term, when strategies are used within an Intervention Framework, the intention is that these will eventually become part of the intervention 'toolkit' (i.e. standard strategies used on a day-to-day basis) and thus become part of the 'Green' foundations or best practice. For ease of use, a coloured Planning Flowchart is included within the Intervention Framework Record using the traffic light colours to identify which level of intervention is planned (p.90).

Once the general elements of the Intervention Framework are identified via the Planning Flowchart, it is helpful to discuss and record these on the Planning Summary before moving on to the next stage of constructing an Intervention Hierarchy when more detailed planning begins. An example Planning Summary is set out in Table 4.1, and a blank copy is included in the Intervention Record pack (p.91).

The Planning Flowchart and the Planning Summary are used to identify which elements are needed within intervention planning, but the next step in the planning stage is to set out how the plan will be implemented:

Table 4.1 Planning Summary example

FOUNDATIONS – Environment? General strategies? Communication?   A distraction-free environment with a separate area for individual work. Regular sensory breaks (swing). Use of pictures and artefacts to introduce new topics. Use of a visual timetable.
NEW SKILLS TO BE TAUGHT – How?   To request help. Use of a help card. Initial hand over hand prompt on behaviour signal that help is needed and reduce/fade prompt as skill develops.
REWARDS OR REINFORCING ACTIVITIES – How are these to be used?   Use of 'this first – then this' card. Using preferred activities (drawing and colouring, books) to follow less favoured activities (maths, PE).
AMBER STRATEGIES – Functionally Equivalent Behaviour OR Diversion? – Details   When showing an emerging need for a sensory break (gentle rocking) divert with a sensory break card and 5 mins swing time.
RED STRATEGIES – Details   If shouting and rolling on the floor (need for sensory break missed). Show Red signal by saying 'stop' and asking X to sit (support with sign and symbol) as soon as sitting and calm (even for 1 second!). Re-focus to choose sensory break card (no sensory break until calm and card presented).

- When and how to reward?

- When and how to divert?

- What action or strategy should be used at the Red stage?

This is done using the Intervention Hierarchy.

Step 2 – Using the Intervention Hierarchy

When facing behaviour which is challenging (in whatever form!) it is often hard to decide when to ignore, when to divert and when or whether to carry out a specific action. As within the Prioritizing process, the Intervention Hierarchy (p.92) uses a traffic light system to separate the differing strategies and link their use to the severity or type of behaviour occurring. Information gained from all earlier stages of the 5P Approach is used for this.

The Intervention Hierarchy is used to plan the actions and approaches to be used within the intervention plan and also to define boundaries. The use of an intervention hierarchy is particularly helpful when behaviour occurs in a sequence of different actions or when the level or severity of a behaviour changes, for example, a light tap changing to hitting (as highlighted within the A BBB C process). The hierarchy provides a mechanism for using different strategies at different levels of severity and so promotes a proactive approach to behaviour intervention. Using the hierarchy also provides a way to ensure consistency and continuity of approach amongst individuals involved in behaviour management. Using the distinct colour coding system to describe different behaviours, and then applying strategies to these, allows us to use a simple common language which is clear to all and easily conveyed (i.e. if this is an Amber behaviour – this is the Amber strategy we all use).

Levels of the Intervention Hierarchy

Green level represents where we want to be and where we want to stay, the 'foundations' (see Chapter 2) of good practice where the autism-friendly environment and autism-specific strategies generally prevent behaviour issues arising, where any difficult behaviour which does occur is managed through general everyday strategies and where appropriate or desirable behaviour is rewarded through using intrinsically motivating activities or through use of specific reward systems and strategies. The Green level therefore represents an autism-friendly environment, where all adults have an autism 'toolkit' of strategies to use.

The Amber level represents 'bubbling' signals (or precursors to more difficult behaviour) and relates to the A BBB C observations. Amber behaviour signals that, if there is not some intervention, the situation may deteriorate. Use of strategies at the Amber level therefore aims to catch things before Red behaviour happens, pre-empting and preventing escalation and thus returning to the Green level as soon as possible. It is appropriate at the Amber stage (before a Red behaviour has occurred) to use strategies such as diversion or taking a break (this is explained more fully later in this chapter). The use of Amber strategies serves to promote independence, enabling the child or young person to recognize that when at the early stages of emerging anxiety or anger, a request for a break or support will mean that the problem causing anxiety or anger will be addressed and overcome and things will return to normal (a return to Green).

The use of a less supportive approach with action at the Red stage gives a clear signal that there is a difference between 1) recognizing when things are going wrong and using strategies to overcome any problems and 2) when things have 'gone too far' and there are then consequences which are not so supportive. The aim in all cases is to remain at or return to Green as quickly as possible. Red strategies act as signals *not* as punishments (see below).

The Intervention Hierarchy — Where to start?

We start by using the traffic light system as set out in the Intervention Hierarchy sheet with everyone involved in the discussion and decision making about which level to place particular behaviours and which strategies to use for these. Once decisions are made about which behaviours are to be placed at each level, these descriptions are recorded on the sheet.

The following questions can be used as a guide to aid the decision-making process. You will have already collected some of this information on the Planning Summary sheet.

- Which behaviours can be ignored or dealt with within the current everyday approach (i.e as part of the foundations)? These tend to be low level behaviours which have no *significant* impact. These are recorded at Green 1 level on the chart.

- Which behaviours would you like to see increased or developed (i.e. behaviours to reward, often those which prevent difficult behaviours arising)? These are recorded at Green 2 level on the sheet. Question: Does this involve teaching new skills? If so you will need to consider the method you will use to teach these and also link to a reward system if appropriate (see Chapter 5).

- Which behaviours cannot be ignored (i.e need to change or be prevented) but do not need an immediate action or Red signal? This level includes 'bubbling' signals (i.e. behaviours which have been identified as precursors to more difficult or extreme behaviour (Red) via the A BBB C chart). These are placed at the Amber level. You will need to consider whether to encourage a functionally equivalent behaviour (FEB), a behaviour which serves the same purpose, or whether to plan to divert. More information on how to decide which to use is set out later in this chapter.

- Behaviours placed at the Red level are those which are agreed by all involved to be those which cannot be left or tolerated and require an immediate action. Actions which cause harm to self or others are *always* Red.

Note: although now at a different stage of prioritizing, the Prioritizing activities and materials described earlier can also be used to help 'sort' behaviours into the different levels.

Here is an example of how the Intervention Hierarchy might work. The information we have gained so far is as follows. The behaviour identified for intervention is that the child pinches. The identified function of the behaviour is that it is primarily a sensory need but is also multifunctional. This pinching also becomes a signal that the child is becoming very anxious (but changes to hard pinching) and that he or she needs a sensory break to help regain a calm status. The proposed Intervention Hierarchy is therefore as detailed in Table 4.2.

The Intervention Hierarchy chart sets this out using the colour coded system and also sets out more detail in relation to strategies to be used at each level. A coloured, blank, photocopiable Intervention Hierarchy chart is included within the Intervention Framework Record pack (p.92).

Deciding which strategies to use at which level

Green 1 level strategies are those which are used as part of the everyday 'toolkit' and established within the foundations of good practice. Such strategies might include ignoring, the use of a picture cue, a simple verbal reminder, diversion, etc.

Green 2 level strategies include any reward system used and new skills to be taught. Rewarding appropriate behaviour (or behaviour which has been targeted to be increased or taught) can take many forms, from using teaching activities which are intrinsically rewarding or activities followed by a rewarding activity (best practice) to complex token-based reward systems. The nature of any formal reward system depends on the child or young person's level of understanding but, as a rule of thumb, the simplest reward system should be used in the first instance. Many individuals with more severe forms of ASD, or who may have additional learning difficulty, lack the skills and level of understanding to benefit from a complex reward system. Intrinsically motivating activities or naturally occurring rewards or reinforcers are therefore most powerful in these circumstances. Further guidance on the use of reward systems can be found in Chapter 5. As new skills to be taught have been identified as part of this current intervention, achieving a new skill should, in most cases, be intrinsically rewarding or have a naturally occurring reinforcer built in to the activity or function (i.e. learn to finish a task before break time).

Strategies used at Amber level are linked to the information gained from the Profile and the Problem Solving stage. These are used to plan an appropriate diversion (to a preferred activity) or plan an appropriate break (e.g. a sensory or movement break). Deciding whether to use

Table 4.2. Intervention Hierarchy example

Level	Behaviour	Proposed action
GREEN 1 Managing with everyday strategies.	An occasional light pinch (gentle touch).	**Ignore** and move away
GREEN 2 (Foundations – good practice) Doing the right thing. Doing well.	The child uses Koosh ball instead of pinching. This serves as a functionally equivalent behaviour i.e. a more appropriate behaviour which serves the same (sensory) function as pinching.	**Reward** – use of praise with facial expression, etc. – using the Koosh ball is intrinsically motivating.
AMBER These are 'bubbling' behaviours which are often precursors to more difficult behaviour.	Frequent or persistent light pinching (bubbling).	**Divert to FEB** e.g. Koosh ball or Blu-Tack or a sensory toy.
RED Behaviour which is not acceptable or over the top. Give a clear **signal** of disapproval and consequence.	A hard pinch.	**Immediate**: A **verbal** and **signed signal** 'no' followed by a short Time Out (10–20 seconds on bean bag) to think and calm. The expected **calm signal** before moving on is Sitting quietly. The **'bridging' activity** (an activity which bridges the gap between the Red action and returning to the original situation (if needed) is a short time (2 mins) with book).

diversion or a functionally equivalent behaviour at Amber is part of the Problem Solving Flowchart completion process. As a first instance however, it is useful to apply a first level Amber strategy – for example, a short reminder of what is to come next. This, on some occasions, may be sufficient to re-focus the child/young person and keep them at Green. However, if the 'bubbling' behaviour is a recognized signal that the child needs a break or diversion or is not successfully diverted by the first level strategy, move straight to the agreed second level Amber strategy. Further guidance in relation to choosing whether to divert or use a functionally equivalent behaviour is set out later in this chapter.

Red strategies or actions serve as signals to the child or young person that this behaviour should not occur. The 5P Approach does not advocate the use of sanctions or punishments for Red (undesirable) behaviours but sees Red strategies as signals which distinguish the consequences of Amber (bubbling or warning) behaviour from the consequences of Red behaviour (when things have gone too far).

In addition to clearly showing the child or young person the difference in consequence between Amber and Red behaviour, the distinction of the two stages – though using three different strategies – serves three main purposes:

1. promoting prevention and de-escalation of behaviour which is challenging

2. teaching skills and establishing understanding

3. promoting independence and empowering the child or young person.

Depending on their level of development/understanding and degree of autism, children and young people with autism may not be able to understand the effect that their behaviour has on others and may not be able to put themselves in others' shoes (Theory of Mind). They may not be able to pick up from tone of voice, facial expression or body language alone that a person is feeling angry or upset about something they have caused; they may not appreciate the consequence of their actions (so they do not know the behaviour is not wanted or appropriate without a 'signal'). By teaching new skills and appropriate behaviour patterns (at Amber and Green levels) as in the 5P Approach, some of these difficulties can be addressed and lead to permanent behaviour change. If a Red behaviour is serving as a means of communication, it is unlikely to stop unless the child or young person has alternative means of communication. If Red behaviour is sensory related, again, it is unlikely to stop without the underlying sensory need being addressed. Therefore, ignoring inappropriate behaviour or letting it continue with the assumption that it will extinguish is unwise. Ignoring behaviour which caused injury to self or others or allowing it to continue unchallenged is similarly unwise and unproductive and frequently unsafe. Apart from the obvious damage to relationships and physical well-being, it offers no means for the child or young person to learn new skills or develop understanding in order to develop independence and the ability to self-regulate their behaviour. Even though we may understand the reason for a Red behaviour occurring and appreciate that there is no intention to offend or hurt, the use of a Red signal (coupled with Amber and Green strategies where appropriate) serves as part of the process of developing understanding of others, understanding of social rules, and independence.

Using a clear and consistent strategy such as a short Time Out or 'robotic' approach (see 'Time Out' section later in this chapter) can provide a distinct signal that the behaviour is not appropriate and is in distinct contrast to the signal given *before* any inappropriate/undesirable behaviour has occurred (when an appropriate behaviour has been used to request help/support/break, etc.). Red strategies are 'cold, calm and quietly' used as a final signal and saved only for those behaviours which have been identified as Red. As such, Red strategies are the 'last resort' with the whole aim of the 5P Approach to prevent Red from occurring. But there is also an acceptance that situations will always arise when Red behaviour occurs, however effective the approach used. The Intervention Hierarchy ensures that the situation returns to Green through a series of steps as soon as possible.

Using Amber strategies — Whether to divert or use a functionally equivalent behaviour

USING A FUNCTIONALLY EQUIVALENT BEHAVIOUR (FEB)

Once the function of a particular behaviour has been identified (i.e. the purpose or what the rewarding element of this is), this information can be used to find another, more appropriate or more effective, behaviour which can replace the unwanted behaviour but which serves the same function (known as a functionally equivalent behaviour or FEB). For example:

- Hitting with the identified function of gaining attention to get needs met is replaced with the FEB of a light tap to gain attention or a verbal signal (using a learned phrase) or using PECS 'I want...', etc.

- Spitting with the identified function of providing a sensory experience is replaced with the FEB of blowing streamers or corn flour and water paste (or 'gloop').

The Problem Solving Flowchart provides a means to identify the function of the behaviour and this information can be used to inform what useful FEBs might be. For a child/young person with identified sensory needs the addition of a sensory profile or involvement of a sensory-trained occupational therapist to give advice on strategies and sensory issues can be very helpful.

It is important to note however that, in some instances, one single behaviour may have multiple functions. In this case there may be a need to identify several FEBs, or intervention strategies may need to be a combination of FEB, diversion and Red actions. These decisions are made within the Intervention Hierarchy process and rely heavily on the information gained within the earlier stages of the 5P Approach. An example of a 'mixed' approach would be the aim of reducing hand flapping where at different levels (depending on the function at the time) the child may be diverted towards a stimulating toy to stop hand flapping (diversion – child's use of hands is incompatible with flapping), diverted to a 'flappy' toy box (FEB – gives an alternative and controlled way of meeting the child's sensory needs) or told 'hands down' (Red – when flapping becomes so severe that it interferes with the individual's access to learning or social opportunities). It is important to remember that any Red strategy should also be accompanied with the use of Green and Amber strategies in order to be effective. This is particularly important with issues such as hand flapping, which may have a high sensory base, as this will not decrease without provision of an alternative opportunity to have sensory needs met.

USING DIVERSION

Some behaviours cannot be replaced with another behaviour which serves the same function, for example, some self-stimulatory behaviours, behaviour which causes an emotional reaction (winds up), verbal behaviour (repetitive questioning, crying, screams, etc.). There may also be situations where using an FEB is not appropriate, for example, when the child uses behaviour to make a request which cannot be met at that time (e.g. wanting snack time or a particular activity). In these cases, the strategy is to divert to an *alternative* activity or divert to a behaviour which is *incompatible* (i.e. stops or conflicts) with the unwanted behaviour.

Examples of diversion to alternative behaviour:

- The child requests a snack at a time when this is not possible. The strategy would be to divert to puzzles using a 'this first – then this' visual representation.

- The child makes a loud noise (which is a precursor to temper tantrum). The strategy would be to divert to 'take a break' or an alternate activity that will distract.

Examples of diversion to an incompatible behaviour:

- The child snatches from others at mealtimes. The strategy would be to divert and reward for 'hands on table'.

- The child runs in school. The strategy would be to divert and reward for good walking on printed footsteps or along a coloured line.

A word of caution: when using a strategy of diverting behaviour it is important to remember the principles of learning theory, that is, that a behaviour which immediately precedes a reward or reinforcement will be repeated. For example, if a child climbs on a table as an (inappropriate) signal that a break is needed and is then diverted straight to 'Take a Break' and play outside, the communication signal for Taking a Break will be learned as climbing on the table. But the behaviour is indicating the need for a break to prevent escalation, so what do we do? In these instances, there are two options:

1. Use an immediate Red action (e.g. a cold, calm and quiet request to get down or a very short period of Time Out) and then follow with a break once the appropriate signal (such as sitting down or using PECS to request) has occurred.

2. Where an immediate Red action is not appropriate, insert a 'signal' behaviour into the routine such as:

   • prompt a calm behaviour (sit down) then, once achieved, schedule to divert or break

   • stop behaviour, prompt to make a request for a break, then break

   • stop behaviour using a visually presented 'no...' card, then divert to alternative behaviour.

Some examples to illustrate this point are shown in Figure 4.2. These examples show how a clear 'signal' can be inserted in the process to ensure that the behaviour immediately preceding a reward is a positive and appropriate one.

Note: The same principle applies when using a Time Out procedure. The Intervention Framework suggests including a signal after Time Out and before moving on, to encourage independent use of the signal to lead to an alternative behaviour (this is expanded further later in this chapter).

Red strategies or Amber strategies?

Red behaviours are those which are considered to be a priority for change and are agreed to be unacceptable and needing immediate intervention. The use of strategies at the Red stage is designed to give a clear signal that boundaries have been crossed. For example, there

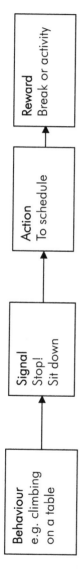

The behaviour immediately preceding the reward (break) is to follow the schedule.

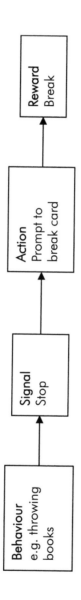

The behaviour immediately preceding the reward (break) is to use the break card.

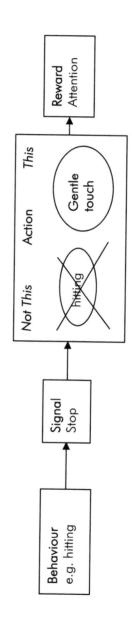

The behaviour immediately preceding the reward (attention) is the gentle touch.

Figure 4.2 Examples consistent with learning theory

is a distinction between when things are getting difficult (Amber) but behaviour, although bubbling, has not yet reached the Red criteria, and there can be a break, relax time, etc., and when the boundaries have been broken (Red) which means a consequence that is not rewarding. It is important to remember that when a function of a behaviour is known, this information is used to inform the strategies which can be used. Identifying the function does not *excuse* unacceptable behaviour – biting or climbing may be identified as a sensory need but biting a person or climbing on furniture still breaks the rules. In the case of climbing, the Amber strategy, used when the child gives a signal that he or she is about to climb (but has not climbed yet), can be to divert to a movement break (e.g. time on the trampoline). The Red strategy (when the child has climbed) would be to give a Red signal such as 'get down [action], sit here [calm signal]', prompt to request a break appropriately, then provide a break.

So, when do you use a Red action and when do you divert (Amber)? The following examples, distinguishing between Time Out (a Red strategy) and Take a Break (an Amber strategy), explain this more fully.

TAKE A BREAK

The use of a short break from an activity is increasingly being used in conjunction with communication systems in order to encourage a child or young person to independently request a break and thus pre-empt behaviour issues arising. For example, teaching a child to request a break is a key feature of the Picture Exchange Communication System (PECS) and Pyramid Approach (Frost and Bondy 1994).

Initially, the child or young person is encouraged to 'Take a Break' when trigger signs for difficult behaviour occur. For example, when a child finds it increasingly difficult to remain in a noisy room, he or she may begin to show an increase in motor mannerisms or place hands over ears – if this is not addressed, it may result in the child running out of the room or having a temper tantrum. The aim is to support the child in recognizing the signs and independently to request a break. This request can be made verbally, with a sign or gesture, via the use of a PECS (visual) symbol or use of a break token or card. In the early stages, the process of teaching the child to request a break may need to use shaping of behaviour using physical or verbal prompts, gradually fading the prompts until the child is able to request independently.

A break should be time limited (the time limit set and made clear right from the start) by use of a timer or 'pinger' or a discrete activity (twice round the playground, two puzzles, etc.). A break should include an activity which the child finds calming, and is used to help the child relax and prepare to re-begin the activity/situation left and not as a sanction. The choice of break activity is determined by looking at the child's Profile and may include a short physical activity, a sensory break (under a blanket, listening to music, looking at pictures, time with a sensory toy) a favourite activity, etc. In some situations, where a forthcoming activity has caused stress, it may be helpful to alter the timetable or schedule by placing a more favourable activity after the break before resuming the original activity or by use of a 'this first – then this' direction showing the child what will follow the next activity.

In some situations, where a child has developed sufficient skills to make choices, a break can be a choice from a 'Break Choice Board' which contains a menu of possible break activities.

Caution: The Take a Break strategy is used to pre-empt or divert difficult situations arising (i.e. at Amber or Green), and should not be used if an inappropriate behaviour has already occurred (at Red). As with the diversion strategies discussed above, it is important to remember the principles of learning theory: *a behaviour which immediately precedes a reward or reinforcement will be repeated.* If a Red behaviour occurs, then a Red strategy should be applied, and once a suitable 'calm signal' has occurred it is then appropriate to move to the Amber strategy or break (as it follows an appropriate behaviour).

TIME OUT

Time Out is the removal of a child from a particular situation to spend a short time isolated from the current situation. Time Out is a procedure commonly used as a 'thinking time' to discourage behaviour which is rewarding a child in some way (i.e. giving attention, either positive or negative). For children with autism and related disorders, removal from attention may not be understood. However, a very short removal from the situation acts as a clear signal that a particular behaviour is not wanted and not appropriate. The aim in using a Time Out process in conjunction with a Take a Break system is to help the child to appreciate the difference between following a path which prevents difficulties occurring (Taking a Break with an enjoyable activity) and following a path which is not acceptable (Time Out – time away from enjoyable activities). Time Out is traditionally time taken in a particular area (e.g. stairs, room or chair). A child is taken or sent to Time Out with a brief verbal or pictorial signal to explain what he or she has done (e.g. no hitting, no spitting, etc.). A child leaves the Time Out area when the behaviour has stopped and when the child has given a clear signal that he or she is calm and ready to return to the original situation. The length of time spent in Time Out will vary according to the child and the situation but should be as short as practicable. In the early stages of establishing a Time Out routine, it may be necessary to 'shape' the Time Out behaviour, beginning with just a few seconds and extending as the child follows the routine. It may also be helpful to use a visually based 'Time Out routine schedule' which gives a pictorial representation of the process, such as that in Figure 4.3.

Time Out

Sit

Think/count to 10/take deep breaths, etc.

Wait

Next activity (from schedule or transition activity – it is important that the next activity is more rewarding than Time Out!)

Figure 4.3 The Time Out process

The Time Out schedule can be placed in the area used for Time Out (laminated or out of reach!) ready for use when Time Out occurs. Where this routine is not possible (because the child is very young, the level of understanding is poor or the process exacerbates behaviour and is too difficult to manage consistently), Time Out can also be time away from adult attention by brief removal of eye contact, turning away, etc. (being a 'robot', cold, calm and quiet). A brief signal ('stop' with a sign) preceding this will serve to indicate that this is 'disapproval' and will distinguish Red action from diversion.

How do you decide – Take a Break or Time Out? This takes us back to learning theory again. Take a Break is used *before* an unacceptable behaviour occurs (at the 'bubbling' stage) with the intention of preventing or diverting and pre-empting difficult behaviour and encouraging the child to develop independent (self) behaviour management skills. A break should always be preceded by a positive signal – a request or instruction following appropriate 'signal' behaviour. The request for a break may need to be shaped, initially with lots of adult prompting, gradually decreasing prompts as the child becomes independent in requesting a break. Time Out (or a Red action) is used *after* an inappropriate behaviour has occurred and gives a clear signal that the behaviour is not acceptable. Red actions used should be appropriate to the child or young person and the situation and can be very brief (see above) as long as they serve the purpose of giving a signal and distinguishing unacceptable behaviour. A Red action or Time Out is not a punishment!

Other Red actions / strategies

A Red action can also be loss of reward or delay of rewarding activity (e.g. waiting to calm before next activity). This would occur naturally as a consequence of leaving Green. 'Natural' consequences tend to be the most powerful in supporting behaviour change. A natural consequence would be one which follows moving away from an appropriate behaviour, for example, shoes off means no playtime (until shoes are on).

SANCTIONS AND PUNISHMENTS

The 5P Approach does not advocate the use of sanction or punishment as part of the Red stage. In very few cases however a small sanction *may* be considered as a 'cost' response to particular behaviour which occurs. Any sanction or punishment *must* be carefully considered in relation to the age of the child/young person and their level of understanding and awareness of the consequences of their actions, and used only after other strategies have been tried as part of a wider intervention package. If the Green and Amber strategies are working well, there should be little need for any Red strategy or sanction. All Red strategies or consequences should be immediate (i.e. directly after a Red behaviour has occurred), short and used as part of an overall approach which promotes and rewards appropriate behaviour.

Step 3 – Constructing the Intervention Framework

The final step of the Planning stage is to set out *how* all the elements come together to make a cohesive plan which can be applied consistently to maximize the potential for behaviour change. This forms the final Intervention Framework. The overall intervention plan is recorded on the Intervention Framework Flowchart which provides a visual representation of the whole plan, all its elements and how it fits together.

Using the Intervention Framework Flowchart

Having identified the elements needed within the plan via the Planning Flowchart (p.90) and the Planning Summary (p.91) and the behaviours and strategies which should be placed at the Green, Amber and Red levels using the Intervention Hierarchy (p.92), the Intervention Framework Flowchart (p.93) is then completed step by step. This flowchart is used to provide an immediate visual representation of the overall framework which:

- sets out clear guidance for all involved in the intervention process

- shows visually the connection between Green, Amber and Red phases and how they interact

- ensures a systematic and consistent approach

- provides opportunities for the child/young person to develop independence in managing behaviour

- places emphasis on a process which always returns to Green.

The Intervention Framework Flowchart has blank spaces in which to record the agreed intervention strategies as set out in the previous planning documents. Before completing the flowchart, it is useful to 'walk through' the process, beginning with the Green levels. The completed Intervention Framework can then be displayed for all to see.

As an overall summary of strategies and process in one document, the Intervention Framework Flowchart is, by necessity, complex. It is useful therefore to place the Intervention Hierarchy sheet (which provides a quick reminder) next to the completed Intervention Flowchart. These two together will provide an instant visual summary of the overall intervention plan.

An example of a completed Intervention Framework Flowchart is set out in Figure 4.4 and a blank copy (coloured in the distinct traffic light colours for ease of use) can be found in the Intervention Framework Record (p.93).

Implementation

The Intervention Framework Flowchart and Intervention Hierarchy also provide guidance for the implementation of the strategies at each level (or colour). Starting with the relevant colour, the flowchart shows a clear pathway to follow. Using the flowchart in this way maximizes the consistency of approach for individuals and also between all adults involved with the intervention process. It also emphasises the relationship between the three levels (Green, Amber and Red) and the way in which all paths finally lead back to Green. Using this framework, the focus is on maintaining 'Green' whenever possible – if there is a need to move to Amber, the focus is on getting back to Green and the main aim is to keep any move to Red at a minimum (which will happen if the Green and Amber strategies are applied consistently). Nonetheless, there will almost always be times when a Red behaviour occurs and action needs to be taken. Working through the pathway from Red

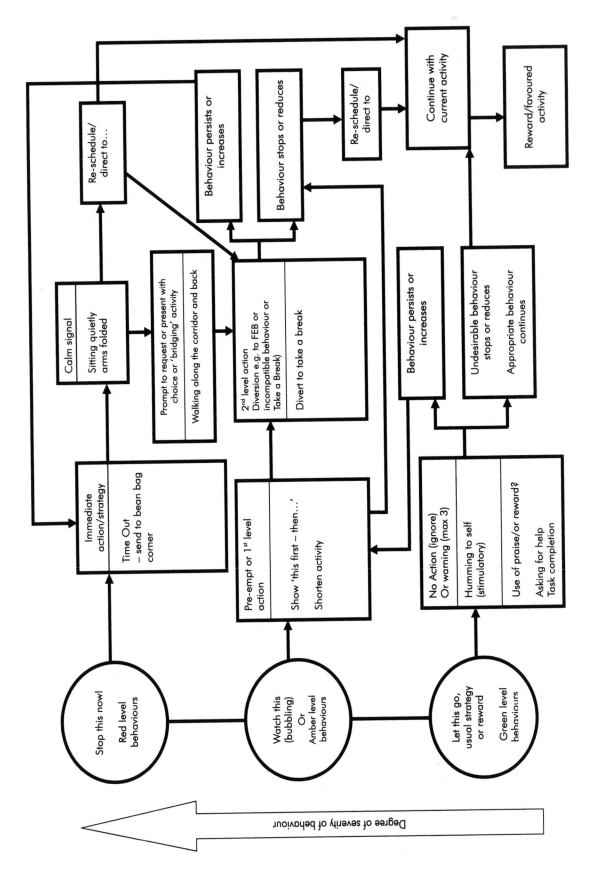

Figure 4.4 Intervention Framework Flowchart example

ensures that things are brought back to 'normal' (Green) as soon as possible.

Caution: It is important to monitor and evaluate the Intervention Framework on a regular basis and adjust as needed. For example, if using a strategy of ignoring a behaviour in Green always leads to moving up the Intervention Hierarchy, this behaviour will need to be moved to Amber or Red. Similarly, as Amber strategies become established as part of the routine, they will become Green strategies and be absorbed into the foundations of good practice.

Making a start! Working through the 5P Approach – step by step

Although individual elements of the 5P Approach can be used without going through all the stages, this is best done once you have become really familiar with all the stages and materials available. The easiest way to begin is to simply work through the process one stage at a time using the 5P Checklist as a guide. Even though you may know the child or young person very well and have a good idea about the underlying function of the behaviour you want to address, completing the Profile, Prioritizing and Problem Analysis stages is still useful and may provide a different viewpoint or additional information which can really make a difference to the success or failure of the intervention plan.

To make it easier to follow the whole process from start to finish, the essential records are put together in an Intervention Framework Record pack. The pack contains all the information gathered from the five stages and makes a useful and comprehensive summary of the whole process. Although the pack itself is useful for the child or young person's file, for implementation just the Planning Summary, the Intervention Hierarchy and the Intervention Framework Flowchart need be displayed (on the wall for example) as they contain the major elements of the intervention plan and strategies to be followed.

The 5P Approach Checklist can be found at the beginning of the Intervention Framework Record pack (p.84) and provides an easy way to track progress through all the stages.

The Intervention Framework Record pack which follows on pages 83–97 contains the following:

- Front cover sheet
- The 5P Approach checklist
- Profile
- Intervention Priority Sorting sheet
- A BBB C chart
- Problem Solving Flowchart
- Problem Solving Summary sheet
- Planning Flowchart
- Planning Summary
- Intervention Hierarchy
- Intervention Framework Flowchart.

Chapter 5 contains additional materials which may be added to the Record, including:

- Observation Record sheets
- Discussion Summary and Prompt sheet
- Teaching New Skills Record sheet
- Reward Record sheet

Note: The four colour pages which follow after the Record pack are for use with strategies explained in Chapter 6.

The 5P Approach
Intervention Framework
Record
for

The 5P Approach Profile

Name:

Completed by:

Date:

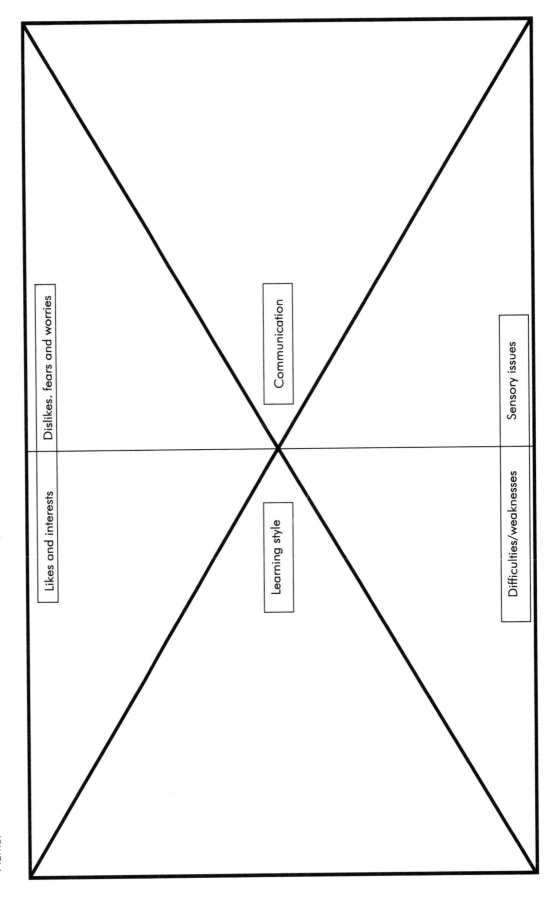

Likes and interests

Dislikes, fears and worries

Communication

Learning style

Sensory issues

Difficulties/weaknesses

The 5P Approach Intervention Priority Sorting sheet

Name: Date:

Completed by:

Sort identified behaviours into priority categories below
(small Post-it notes are ideal for this!)

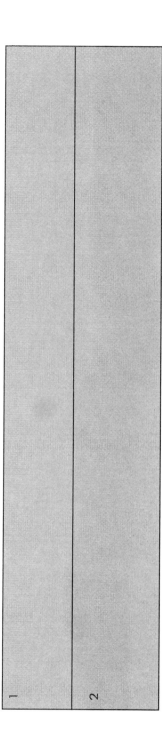

Red Level
Requires immediate action

Amber Level
Needs addressing but can wait
or can be diverted

Green 1 Level
I can live with this!
(no specific action)

Green 2 level
Behaviour which can be
increased or developed

The 5P Approach A BBB C chart

Name: Completed by: Date:

Overall description of behaviour:

Antecedent	Behaviour			Consequence
A	B	B	B	C

The 5P Approach Problem Solving Flowchart

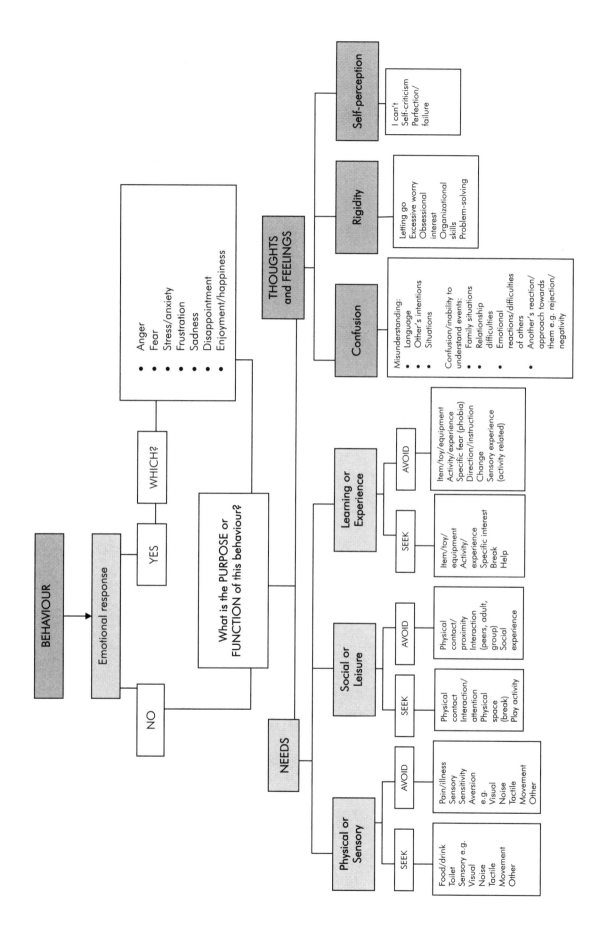

The 5P Approach Problem Solving Summary sheet

Name:

Completed by: Date:

From the Problem Analysis Stage – what do we know about the problem? (using information from A BBB C, observation and discussion)

Antecedent – what led to this?	Behaviour – description	Consequence – what was the result?
	Stage One – early warning signs	
	Stage Two – 'bubbling' behaviour	
	Stage Three – final stage behaviour	

Problem-solve – Hypothesis – why is the problem occuring? (From the Problem Solving Flowchart)

What is the purpose of the behaviour?

Record your statement/hypothesis below:

The 5P Approach Planning Flowchart

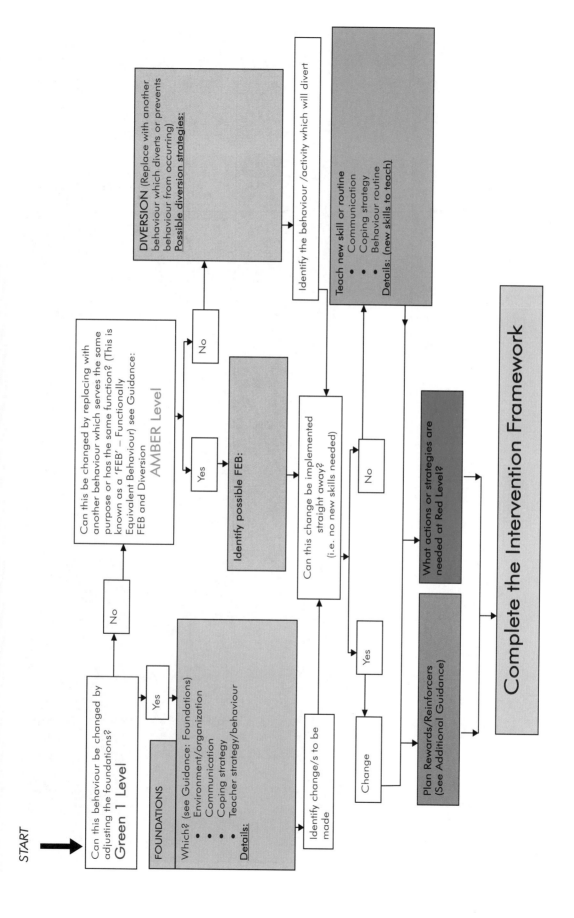

START

Green 1 Level
Can this behaviour be changed by adjusting the foundations?

No

AMBER Level
Can this be changed by replacing with another behaviour which serves the same purpose or has the same function? (This is known as a 'FEB' – Functionally Equivalent Behaviour) see Guidance: FEB and Diversion

Yes

No

DIVERSION (Replace with another behaviour which diverts or prevents behaviour from occurring) <u>Possible diversion strategies:</u>

Identify possible FEB:

Identify the behaviour /activity which will divert

Teach new skill or routine
- Communication
- Coping strategy
- Behaviour routine

<u>Details: (new skills to teach)</u>

Yes

FOUNDATIONS

Which? (see Guidance: Foundations
- Environment/organization
- Communication
- Coping strategy
- Teacher strategy/behaviour

<u>Details:</u>

Identify change/s to be made

Can this change be implemented straight away? (i.e. no new skills needed)

No

Yes

Change

Plan Rewards/Reinforcers (See Additional Guidance)

What actions or strategies are needed at Red Level?

Complete the Intervention Framework

The 5P Approach Planning Summary

Name: Completed by: Date:

| FOUNDATIONS – Environment? General strategies? Communication? |
| NEW SKILLS TO BE TAUGHT – How? |
| REWARDS OR REINFORCING ACTIVITIES – How are these to be used? |
| AMBER STRATEGIES – FEB OR DIVERSION? – Details |
| RED STRATEGIES - Details |

The 5P Approach Intervention Hierarchy

Name   Date:

Completed by:

What behaviour?	What strategy?	
Red Level behaviour Not acceptable Over the top Clear signal of disapproval – consequence	Red action: Calm signal expected: 'Bridging' activity if needed	
Amber Level behaviour 'bubbling' behaviour Pre-cursors to more difficult behaviour Divert and distract, break	First Level: (pre-empt) Second Level (e.g. divert or break?)	
Green Level behaviour (Foundations - good practice) Doing the right thing Doing well GREEN 1	Reward…	
Ignoring or managing with everyday strategies GREEN 2		

The 5P Approach Intervention Framework Flowchart

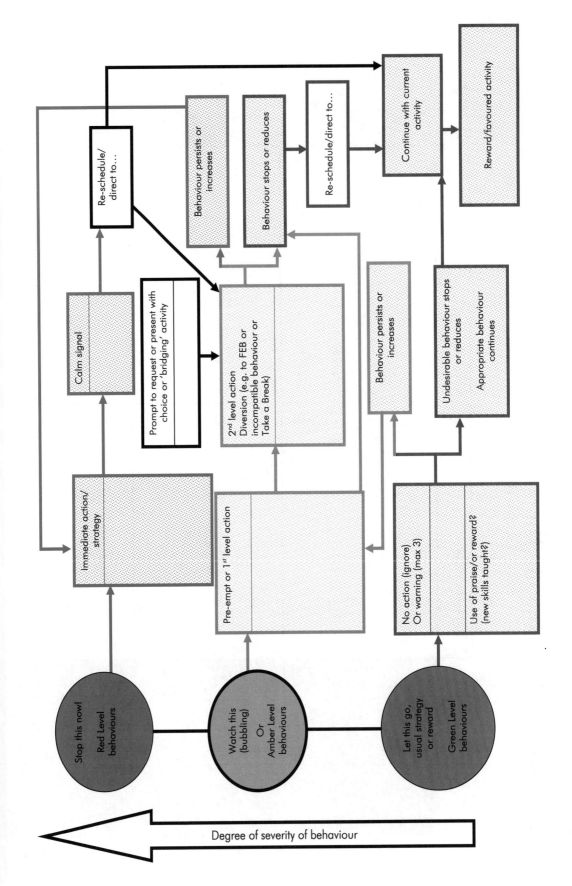

My Traffic Lights

Name:

Completed by:

Date:

Green behaviours

I get a reward for these:

Amber behaviours

I need help, this is what I do:

Red behaviours

Red light behaviours mean:

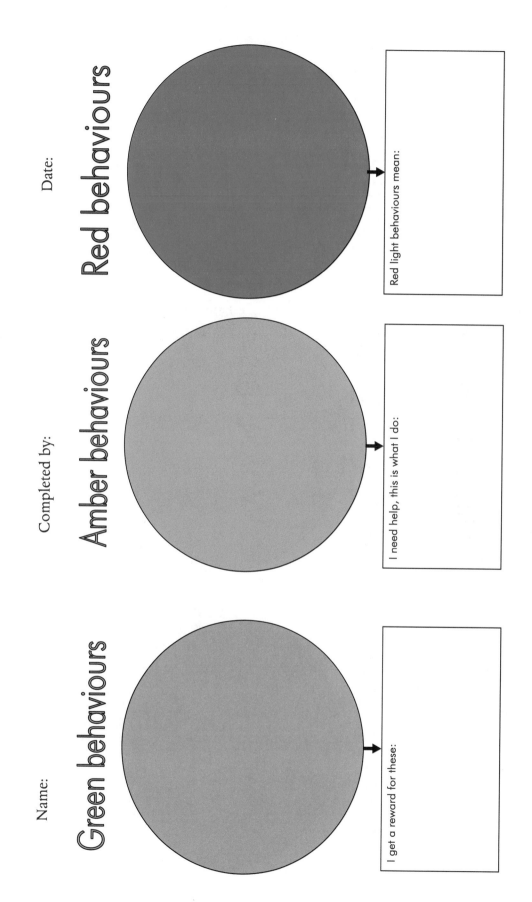

Traffic Light Signals

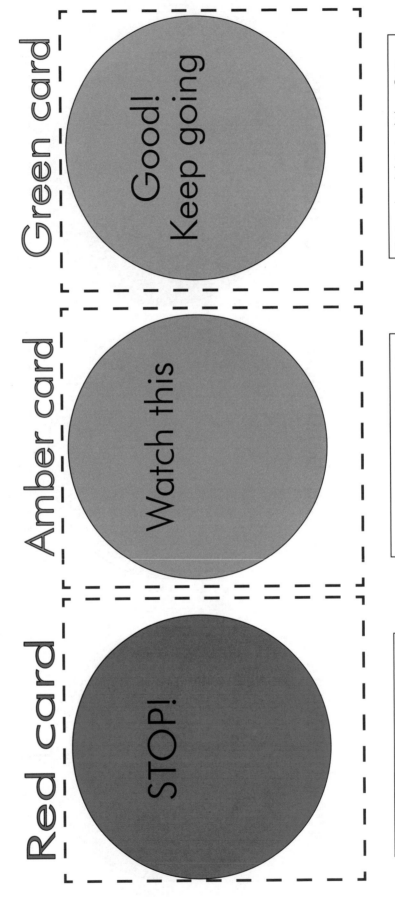

Red card

STOP!

This is used immediately to signal when a Red behaviour has occurred. This signals a move straight to agreed Red strategy e.g. TIME OUT. The Intervention Framework process is then followed to move through Amber and back to Green.

Amber card

Watch this

This is used immediately to signal that an Amber behaviour has occurred. Move straight to the agreed Amber strategy e.g. a verbal reminder and diversion. Then follow the Intervention Framework process back to Green.

Green card

Good! Keep going

This is used regularly to signal when a Green behaviour has occurred. (NB. This does not include ignored behaviour – which is ignored!) Follow agreed Green reward strategy e.g. praise, stickers, rewarding activity, etc.

Feelings management – child/young person

Name:

Completed by:

Date:

	Step 1 – What behaviour?	Step 2 – What strategy?
Red Level behaviour **HELP!**		
Amber Level behaviour My 'bubbling' behaviour I need to watch this!		
Green Level behaviour I'm OK!		

Getting worried? Getting angry?

Managing my feelings and behaviour

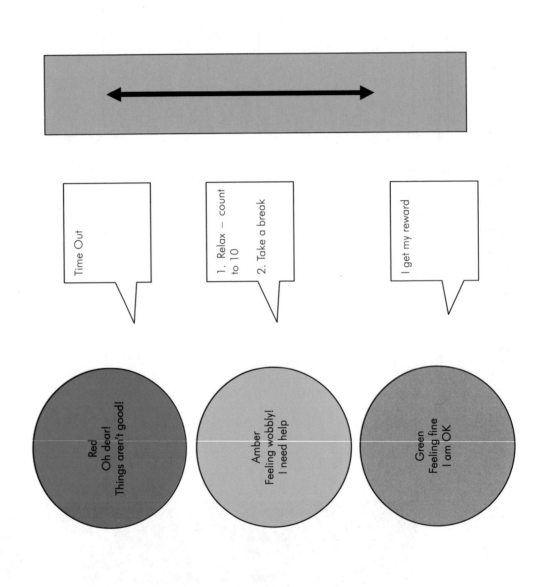

The 5P Approach Intervention Framework checklist

Name: Date:

Completed by:

Please tick	5P Stage	Intervention Process	Relevant 5P documentation	Date completed
	1	PROFILE completed	5P Profile	
	2	PRIORITIES identified	5P Priority Sorting sheet	
			Why change behaviour? checklist	
	3	PROBLEM ANALYSIS completed	Problem Analysis – describing behaviour	
		• A BBB C chart	5P A BBB C chart	
		• Observation notes	5P Observation guidelines and frameworks (Additional guidance)	
		• Discussions with key individuals	5P Discussion summary sheet (Additional guidance)	
	4	PROBLEM SOLVING completed		
		• Problem Solving Flowchart completed	5P Problem Solving Flowchart	
		• Problem Solving Summary/ hypothesis	5P Problem Solving Summary sheet	
	5	PLANNING completed		
		• Planning Flowchart completed	5P Planning Flowchart	
		• Summarise elements needed	5P Planning Summary	
		Intervention Framework		
		• Intervention Hierarchy completed	5P Intervention Hierarchy sheet	
		• Reward system planned and agreed	5P Reward guidance and recording frameworks (Additional guidance)	
		• Teaching new skills and routines planned	5P Teaching new skills guidance and recording frameworks (Additional guidance)	
		• Intervention Framework Flowchart completed	5P Intervention Framework Flowchart	

Additional Guidance and Supporting Materials

This chapter contains additional guidance and materials which support the Problem Analysis and Planning phases of the 5P Approach giving more detail and specific information. The chapter contains the following:

- Observation guidelines and frameworks

- Discussion summary and prompt sheet

- Teaching new skills and routines – guidance and recording frameworks

- Reward guidance and recording frameworks.

Observation guidelines and frameworks

Wherever possible, observation of the focus behaviour, preferably in differing situations or contexts (if this happens), should be part of the initial information gathering for Problem Analysis. As it is difficult to observe and also be part of a situation, observations should be carried out by a third person not involved in the situation where the behaviour is occuring. If this is not possible, the use of video can provide observation material which can be studied later.

General observations

General observations are useful in giving an overall picture of the situation in which behaviour occurs. In addition to looking at specific behaviours in detail to provide information to complete the A BBB C chart, general information can also look at circumstances (e.g. the type of activity), environment (including possible sensory factors) and interaction (with peers and adults). This information detail can be used within all stages of the 5P Approach including planning intervention strategies and altering the environment (changing the foundations).

The General Observation record takes the form of a running record. See Tables 5.1 (example) and 5.2 (blank copy). Using timed intervals (suggested five minutes), there are spaces to quickly record both notes on direct observations and brief comments. The record also has a suggested key to aid shorthand!

Specific observations

In some cases, it is useful to collect information which can be used to monitor and evaluate the success of planned intervention. Structured observations can be used for this purpose and provide a numerical record upon which to plot progress.

Structured observations can collect information on:

- the frequency at which a behaviour occurs (frequency)

- the length of time of a behaviour (duration)

- the presence or absence of a behaviour (interval).

FREQUENCY COUNTS

Simply count the number of times any behaviour occurs within a given period (usually shortened to minutes for ease of counting). This type of observation is best used when behaviours are discrete (i.e. single, short in nature, e.g. a hit or spit or shout, etc.) The Frequency Count records are divided into single and multiple count sheets (Tables 5.3, 5.4, 5.5, 5.6). These are simple systems where the observer is required to make a mark each time the identified behaviour occurs within a given interval.

The counts are then totalled and calculated as frequency per minute (or time unit used). The multiple counts sheet is constructed so that up to three behaviours can be counted at one time.

DURATION OBSERVATIONS

Record the length of time for which a targeted behaviour occurs within a given time period (a stop watch is needed for this!). This type of observation is best used when behaviour occurs over time (e.g. being off task, crying, tantrum, etc.) See Tables 5.7 and 5.8.

INTERVAL OBSERVATIONS

Simply record the presence or absence of a given behaviour within a time slot (usually seconds rather than minutes). This type of observation falls between frequency and duration counts and tends to provide less detailed information. However, this observation can be useful in situations where the targeted behaviour is prolonged, such as constant occurrence of motor mannerisms, rocking, etc. See Tables 5.9 and 5.10.

The first thing to do when using observations to monitor and evaluate progress is to observe and collect data before the planned intervention begins, thus establishing a baseline upon which to measure progress.

The same information is then collected at regular intervals during the intervention period. The frequency of the monitoring is agreed during the Planning phase.

Completed examples and blank copies of recording sheets which can be used for observations can be found on the following pages (Tables 5.1 to 5.10).

Discussion Summary and Prompt Sheet

This pro forma (Table 5.11) can be used as an aide-memoire in discussion with key individuals who have concerns about behaviour or it can be completed by hand and kept as a record. Although not intended to be a formal script, it does give clear areas for discussion and the

Table 5.1 General Observation – running record example

Name:

Completed by:

Date:

Situation observed (Activity, Environment, etc.):

Target behaviour:

Time (in intervals)	Observation notes	Comments (including environmental)
e.g. 5 mins	*General notes / record of exactly what is observed during the time period*	*Record comments which add information or explanation to what is observed*
10 mins		
15 mins		

Shorthand symbols if needed:

OT	On task	+ I	+ve interaction	V	Verbal	+ B	+ve behaviour
→	towards	– I	-ve interaction	**Phy**	Physical	– B	-ve behaviour

Table 5.2 General Observation – running record

Name:

Completed by:

Date:

Situation observed (Activity, Environment, etc.):

Target behaviour:

Time (in intervals)	Observation notes	Comments (including environmental)

Shorthand symbols if needed:

OT	On task	+ I	+ve interaction	V	Verbal	+ B	+ve behaviour
→	towards	- I	-ve interaction	Phy	Physical	– B	-ve behaviour

Table 5.3 Observation – frequency of behaviour recording sheet example (single)

Name: Completed by: Date:

Target behaviour	e.g. biting
Total observation period:	e.g. 20 minutes

Unit time	Frequency count
	Mark each time behaviour occurs e.g. ||/|
e.g. 5 mins	|||
5 mins	||/|
5 mins	||/| ||/|
5 mins	

Total target behaviour: e.g. 20

Time: *e.g. 22 mins*

Frequency per (timescale *e.g. minutes*): *22 per 20 mins*

= 22/20 per min

= 1.1 per min

Table 5.4 Observation – frequency of behaviour recording sheet (single)

Name: Completed by: Date:

Target behaviour	
Total observation period:	

Unit time	Frequency count												

Total target behaviour: Frequency per (timescale *e.g. minutes*):

Time:

Table 5.5 Observation – frequency of behaviour example (multiple)

Name: Completed by: Date:

Target behaviour	
1	Hitting
2	Tapping head
3	Throwing
Total observation period:	20 mins

Unit time	Frequency count		
	1	2	3
5 mins	IIII	I	III
5 mins	I	II	I
5 mins	II	I	
5 mins	III	I	I
	10	5	5

Total behaviours	
1	10
2	5
3	5
Total time taken:	20 mins

Frequency per time (min) 10/20 = 0.5 per min
Frequency per time (min) 5/20 = 0.25 per min
Frequency per time (min) 5/20 = 0.25 per min

Copyright © Linda Miller 2009

Table 5.6 Observation – frequency of behaviour recording sheet (multiple)

Name: Completed by: Date:

Target behaviour	1		
	2		
	3		

Total observation period:

Frequency count			
Unit time	1	2	3

Total behaviours	1	Frequency per time (min)
	2	Frequency per time (min)
	3	Frequency per time (min)

Total time taken:

Table 5.7 Observation – duration of behaviour example

Name: Completed by: Date:

Target behaviour	Rocking
Total time period:	20 mins

Interval	Duration 1	Duration 2	Duration 3	Duration 4	Duration 5
5 mins	Record length of time each behaviour occurs e.g. 10 secs	5 secs	40 secs	25 secs	20 secs
	12 secs	15 secs	35 secs	10 secs	13 secs
5 mins	18 secs	10 secs	45 secs	10 secs	12 secs
5 mins	20 secs	25 secs	20 secs	15 secs	15 secs
5 mins					
Total observation time: 20 mins	Total target behaviour duration: e.g 60 secs	55 secs	140 secs	60 secs	60 secs

Total target behaviour duration: 375 secs (60 + 55 + 140 + 60 + 60)

Percentage target time: total behaviour duration × 100 = $\dfrac{375 \times 100}{1200}$ = 31.25%
Total time

Period (total time): 20 mins (1200 secs)

Table 5.8 Observation – duration of behaviour recording sheet

Name: Date:

Completed by:

Target behaviour	
Total time period:	

Interval	Duration 1	Duration 2	Duration 3	Duration 4	Duration 5
Total observation time:	Total target behaviour duration:				

Total target behaviour duration:

Percentage target time: total behaviour duration × 100 =

Total time

Period (total time):

Table 5.9 Observation – interval example

Name: Date:

Target behaviour: Crying   Completed by:

Record presence (+) of the behaviour per unit of time

Total interval e.g. 150 sec (2.5 min)	Unit 1 (15 sec per unit)	Unit 2 (15 sec)	Unit 3 (15 sec)	Unit 4 (15 sec)	Unit 5 (15 sec)	Unit 6 (15 sec)	Unit 7 (15 sec)	Unit 8 (15 sec)	Unit 9 (15 sec)	Unit 10 (15 sec)
2.5 min	+ 0	+ 0	+ 0	+ 0	+ 0	+ 0	+ 0	+ 0	+ 0	+ 0
2.5 min	+ 0	+ 0	+ 0	+ 0	+ 0	+ 0	+ 0	+ 0	+ 0	+ 0
2.5 min	+ 0	+ 0	+ 0	+ 0	+ 0	+ 0	+ 0	+ 0	+ 0	+ 0
2.5 min	+ 0	+ 0	+ 0	+ 0	+ 0	+ 0	+ 0	+ 0	+ 0	+ 0
2.5 min	+ 0	+ 0	+ 0	+ 0	+ 0	+ 0	+ 0	+ 0	+ 0	+ 0
2.5 min	+ 0	+ 0	+ 0	+ 0	+ 0	+ 0	+ 0	+ 0	+ 0	+ 0
2.5 min	+ 0	+ 0	+ 0	+ 0	+ 0	+ 0	+ 0	+ 0	+ 0	+ 0
2.5 min	+ 0	+ 0	+ 0	+ 0	+ 0	+ 0	+ 0	+ 0	+ 0	+ 0
2.5 min	+ 0	+ 0	+ 0	+ 0	+ 0	+ 0	+ 0	+ 0	+ 0	+ 0
2.5 min	+ 0	+ 0	+ 0	+ 0	+ 0	+ 0	+ 0	+ 0	+ 0	+ 0
2.5 min	+ 0	+ 0	+ 0	+ 0	+ 0	+ 0	+ 0	+ 0	+ 0	+ 0
Sub-totals	7	6	5	5	4	5	4	6	7	4

Total times behaviour present: (7+6+5+5+4+5+4+6+7+4) = 53

Total intervals: 10 (15 sec each)

Total time period: 30 mins

Total no times present per session: 53

% of time present: total intervals x 100 $= \dfrac{10 \times 100}{53} = 18.9\%$

total present

Key:	
0	*absent*
+	*present*

Table 5.10 Observation – interval recording sheet

Name:

Completed by:

Date:

Target behaviour:

Record presence (+) of the behaviour per unit of time

Interval	Unit 1	Unit 2	Unit 3	Unit 4	Unit 5	Unit 6	Unit 7	Unit 8	Unit 9	Unit 10
	(…sec)	(…sec)	(…sec)	(…sec)	(…sec)	(…sec)	(…sec)	(…sec)	(…sec)	(…sec)
5	+ 0	+ 0	+ 0	+ 0	+ 0	+ 0	+ 0	+ 0	+ 0	+ 0
10	+ 0	+ 0	+ 0	+ 0	+ 0	+ 0	+ 0	+ 0	+ 0	+ 0
15	+ 0	+ 0	+ 0	+ 0	+ 0	+ 0	+ 0	+ 0	+ 0	+ 0
20	+ 0	+ 0	+ 0	+ 0	+ 0	+ 0	+ 0	+ 0	+ 0	+ 0
25	+ 0	+ 0	+ 0	+ 0	+ 0	+ 0	+ 0	+ 0	+ 0	+ 0
30	+ 0	+ 0	+ 0	+ 0	+ 0	+ 0	+ 0	+ 0	+ 0	+ 0
35	+ 0	+ 0	+ 0	+ 0	+ 0	+ 0	+ 0	+ 0	+ 0	+ 0
40	+ 0	+ 0	+ 0	+ 0	+ 0	+ 0	+ 0	+ 0	+ 0	+ 0
45	+ 0	+ 0	+ 0	+ 0	+ 0	+ 0	+ 0	+ 0	+ 0	+ 0
50	+ 0	+ 0	+ 0	+ 0	+ 0	+ 0	+ 0	+ 0	+ 0	+ 0
55	+ 0	+ 0	+ 0	+ 0	+ 0	+ 0	+ 0	+ 0	+ 0	+ 0
60	+ 0	+ 0	+ 0	+ 0	+ 0	+ 0	+ 0	+ 0	+ 0	+ 0
Sub-totals										

Total time period:

Total present:

Total intervals:

Total no times present per session:

% of time present: total intervals x 100 =

total present

Key:	
0	*absent*
+	*present*

Table 5.11 Discussion summary and prompt sheet

Name of child: Completed by: Date:

What strategies (if any) do you currently use? How successful are they?
Behaviour identified for change: Tell me about this child/young person (Use 5P Profile as question prompt and complete)   5P Profile completed?   YES/NO
Describe an incident/time when the behaviour occurs – give an exact example: (Use 5P A BBB C chart as a question prompt and record. Prompt sequence focusing particularly on BBB e.g. how do you know when X is becoming anxious? What does s/he do/say, etc.)
A BBB C chart completed?   YES/NO Does anything prevent this from happening?
What strategies (if any) do you currently use? How successful are they?

content ensures all areas are covered to collect the additional information needed for the Problem Analysis and Problem Solving processes. The questions are posed using the A BBB C chart and the 5P Approach Profile as a guide.

The content of the discussion is as follows:

- the behaviour identified for change

- detailed information about the child or young person

- description in detail of an incident or time when the behaviour occurs (an exact example)

- strategies which work (i.e. Does anything prevent the behaviour from happening?).

Teaching new skills

Teaching a new skill is often a crucial part of the intervention process as it is frequently the learning of a new skill or routine which will replace inappropriate behaviour, provide the child or young person with a skill which reduces the need for inappropriate behaviour or provide a coping strategy. The teaching of new skills is therefore integrated within the intervention process and linked directly to the reward system. Identifying which skill to teach takes place at the beginning of the Planning phase. A decision on *how* to teach identified new skills is also part of this process. Examples of how this can be achieved are discussed here.

Single trial teaching

An effective way of teaching new skills in a structured way is to use a rule-based approach which is based on learning theory (sometimes known as Applied Behaviour Analysis or ABA). This provides a consistent and systematic means of teaching which works with the autistic learning style preference. The simplest type of rule-based teaching is what is known as teaching a 'discrete trial'. This format is most commonly used when the target or objective deals with actions which can 'stand alone' and are not linked to other behaviours. It is also useful when many repetitions are needed in a short time. In this process the child is presented with a task, prompted (shaping) to success and given immediate reward (praise, toy, etc.).

Examples include:

- teaching discrimination (e.g. big/little, between letters, colours or numbers, etc.)

- learning a single action to a cue or direction or prompt, initially (e.g. lining up, going to a seat, etc.)

- copying actions (e.g. wave 'bye bye').

This type of single trial teaching and learning, often termed rote learning, is very common in everyday use within the home and school setting. It is a more systematic and consistent approach, coupled with detailed recording, that turns it into the more formal 'ABA' approach. When using this type of approach, it is important to note the need to generalize quickly to more natural contexts as this type of learning can lead to copying or parroting and to the development of rigid behaviour (rote learned). Generalization and functional use of any skills taught in this way is particularly important with individuals with ASD as rigidity in thinking is part of their diagnostic profile. Nonetheless, use of a rule-based and structured approach also works with the typical autistic learning style. Functional use and application of skills learned through these methods is therefore a crucial part of successful teaching and learning.

This type of direct rule-based skills teaching can also be used when introducing a functionally equivalent behaviour (FEB). For example, if you wish the child to replace spitting with the action of blowing a streamer (identified as a FEB). The adult would intervene as the child signals that he or she is about to spit (at Amber) and quickly physically prompt the child to hold and blow a streamer. This behaviour (or skill) then replaces the original behaviour (spitting). Praise reward accompanies the blowing of the streamer, and the action itself, if functionally equivalent, also provides an intrinsic reward. The use of intrinsic rewards or activities that are rewarding in themselves are a powerful way of motivating and reinforcing learning.

Sequential teaching

The second most commonly used form of rule-based teaching is 'sequential'. Sequential learning involves breaking down a task, activity or behaviour into small steps and then presenting a task, activity or new behaviour one step at a time. This method also uses prompts to 'shape' behaviour. The shaping process involves gradually chaining the steps of a task or behaviour, slowly and systematically adding steps as the child succeeds until the child can complete the whole activity in sequence. Initially the child may need a prompt in order to start off the sequence and a prompt within the sequence at each step. Examples of using this type of approach to teach a new skill within a behaviour intervention programme would include:

- teaching the PECS exchange routine (Frost and Bondy 1994)

- teaching a Take a Break routine

- teaching a relaxation routine.

A key feature within this method is the teacher's ability to break the task down into small achievable steps. This is known as task analysis. Task analysis can be applied to a whole task or part of a task. Task analysis involves the identification of a series of independent steps that comprise a complex task (e.g. brushing teeth, dressing). A decision can be made to teach all or part of the task in sequence. The task analysis provides a list of each of the steps in sequence. The sequence can then be taught by forward or backward sequencing (known as forward or backward chaining).

FORWARD CHAINING

This involves starting the lesson with the first step of the sequence and then providing support for the remaining steps. Each learned step is linked together until the sequence is completed from beginning to end. Forward chaining is best used when each step becomes a cue for the next and no single step in the chain is more reinforcing than the next step (e.g. washing hands – see Figure 5.1).

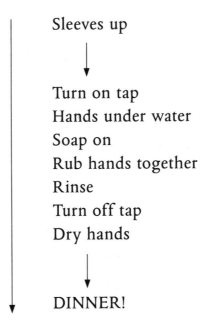

Figure 5.1 Forward chaining behaviour

Forward chains can also be presented in picture form (often called mini schedules or visual jigs).

BACKWARD CHAINING

This involves providing support for all steps until the last step and then teaching the next step. When the last step is mastered the next to last is taught, and so on, until the chain is complete. Backward chaining is best used when the final step results in a significant natural reinforcer that relates to the completion of the entire task (e.g. coat on = playground; shoes on = football).

Prompts

In both of the teaching strategies above, it is likely that in the early stages prompts will need to be used to shape the behaviour and support the development of the skills. The 'teacher' (any adult working with the child or young person) should always use the *minimal* prompt needed to support the child, with the aim of reducing or fading the prompts as soon as the child can complete steps or a task independently.

Prompts can be:

- physical – guiding a hand, steering towards the right seat, etc.

- verbal – verbal instruction or comment

- visual – use of a picture/sign/photo/symbol

- gestural – use of a sign or gesture

- model – modelling by adult.

Rewards, reinforcers or motivators

Rewards, reinforcers or motivators (the terms are usually used synonymously) are often used with rule-based approaches to encourage the establishment of new behaviour (e.g. completion of activities and the following of instructions, etc.). The best rewards are those which *mean* something to the child or young person (i.e. child or young person defined) and in general are practical and concrete in nature. The child or young person should know what reward will follow ('this first – then this' strategy or visual representation/'tempting'). Rewards should be immediate (i.e. directly following the behaviour to be rewarded).

The most effective rewards are the ones which occur naturally throughout the day (e.g. dinner after washing hands, bath after getting undressed, playtime after work time, etc.). When establishing new behaviour or learning a skill, initially it will be necessary to use frequent rewards with the aim of reducing the frequency between rewards or altering the type of reward as soon as practically possible (i.e from reward at each step to reward at the end of the activity, from a toy or food reward to a sticker or praise and cuddle!).

It is important to remember that the use of any reward or reinforcement should be judged on the level of ability and degree of understanding of the child or young person. Complex reward systems which have abstract elements (stickers or tokens) or require a time lapse (working towards a reward) should only be used if the child or young person has the level of understanding (and motivation!) required for their use. Visually presented systems can be an aid to understanding. (See the section on 'Using reward systems' below.)

Recording the teaching of a new skill

A quick reference summary sheet for teaching new skills which incorporates steps (task analysis), prompts and rewards is found in Table 5.12.

First, the complete activity or skill to be taught is recorded on the sheet and then broken down into small, achievable steps. These are listed in sequence on the sheet. The next thing to consider is the teaching format – whether the steps should be taught as a forward or backward chain and the type and amount of prompting that may be needed in the first instance. It is always useful at this stage to also consider how the prompts will be faded or reduced. If the skill to be taught has a built-in reward (i.e. just learning the skill is motivating or brings a reward), there may be no need for any additional reward or motivator. If there is a need for a reward or motivator, consider whether this will just be needed at the end of the task or whether there is a need for smaller rewards or reinforcement at each step. The final thing to consider is how this newly taught skill will be used functionally and how the use of this skill can be generalized into different activites, environments or with different people, etc.

Using reward systems

Using rewards (or reinforcers or motivators) to encourage appropriate behaviour or the development of skills is an essential part of any intervention process and is included within the 5P Approach Intervention Framework at the Green 2 level. However, it is also important to remember that the foundations of good practice should contain activities which are rewarding and motivating in themselves (that is, they should be intrinsically rewarding) by working with the interests of the child or young person and ensuring that the activities presented are practical, functional and meaningful. In this way, the individual is more likely to be engaged with the learning process and motivated to succeed. This type of motivator or reinforcement is far more successful than any 'artificial' reward system, as is any reward which comes naturally as a consequence of the action (e.g. shoes on means playtime, wash hands means lunch, etc.).

Table 5.12 The 5P Approach teaching new skills recording sheet

Name: **Completed by:** **Date:**

*Task/behaviour to be taught:	
Identified steps: 1 2 3 4 5 6 7 8	Teaching format: Forward or backward chain? Reinforcers/rewards/motivators At each step? At end?
** Prompts to be used: 1 2 3	Notes/other information

* Note: use minimal prompts where possible and aim to decrease prompts as soon as possible.

** Aim to promote generalization of skills by giving opportunity to use new skills in a variety of contexts.

As discussed earlier in this book, many children and young people with ASD have problems with Executive Function (planning, organizing and sequencing) which has an effect on their ability to appreciate the passage of time. They therefore often find it difficult to look forward to things which may happen in the future (e.g. a reward at the end of the day). Visual representations of rewards and timetables set out clearly what the final reward or outcome will be and what steps (if any) have to be achieved to get there.

Individuals with ASD often experience difficulty in understanding abstract concepts such as the use of tokens or stickers to represent a more concrete reward. Any system should therefore be carefully planned in consideration of the level of understanding of the child or young person concerned. Similarly, the use of praise or verbal comment can be meaningless to those who do not have understanding of abstract concepts or who might not be able to 'read' tone of voice or facial expression. If this is the case, the adult should not avoid the use of praise and facial expression to accompany more concrete rewards; but should avoid the use of these techniques alone to reinforce appropriate behaviour until the individual develops an appreciation of what these mean. Nonetheless, for many individuals, the use of more complex reward systems, particularly when presented visually, can be an effective and important part of an overall Intervention Framework.

The most effective reward is an immediate one. A small reward can follow desired behaviour and can be visually represented so that the child or young person knows what will come. This can be done in a simple form using a 'This first – then this' card (see examples below). This type of reward is particularly effective when it occurs naturally as part of the routine, for example 'This first (shoes on) then (playtime)'.

Within some behaviour programmes, particularly those where a sequence of behaviour is being taught, a small reinforcer can be used at each stage to aid the shaping process (e.g. praise, a small food reward or token).

Rewards should be used to reward behaviour which has been identified for development or to be increased and this should be identified explicitly giving a clear indication as to what is required (e.g. sitting down, asking for help, etc.). It is not helpful to reward a child for non-specific behaviour such as 'playing nicely' which offers no clear direction as to what behaviour is required (and may need skills to be achieved!). The child or young person may not understand what is required of them or, if they understand what is required, they may not have developed the skills needed to carry this out independently. Neither, for the same reason, is it helpful to reward a child for *not* doing something (e.g. for not hurting or not running out of class).

A visual representation can also be used to show the stages leading towards the final reward or achievement. This also supports understanding in that it gives 'the whole picture' by setting out the start and end points and shows clearly what is expected without ambiguity. Visual representations of stages leading to reward can take many forms and vary in complexity, for example:

- schedules or timetables setting out the process to the end reward or reinforcing activity (e.g. a series of activities ending with lunchtime)

- use of tokens to represent steps (see below)

- use of parts of a picture of the final reward with the reward gained when all parts are collected (see below)

- reward charts.

It is important to match the complexity of the reward system to the level of the child or young person's understanding. Many children and young people with autistic spectrum disorders experience difficulty in understanding abstract concepts. If this is the case, use of stickers or tokens which are collected to purchase rewards may be too hard for them to understand and, as a result, the reward system will have little effect. When choosing rewards or motivators it is also important to make sure that what is offered is indeed motivating for *that individual* even though it may seem appealing to us. Some behaviour approaches use a method of identifying motivators for individuals and setting them out into a hierarchy. This can be useful when very structured teaching takes place or when it is difficult to motivate or engage an individual. The 5P Profile identifies likes and preferences and these should be used as a basis for choosing rewards or reinforcing activities. It is also very important to make sure that the reward you are offering is not so important to the individual that it gets in the way of achieving the task or moving on to the next task. For example, for a child who has an almost obsessive interest in trains, providing this as a reward in the middle of a sequence of activities may be counterproductive as leaving this to move on to another activity will become very stressful and could cause more behaviour issues. The type and timing of rewards used is therefore an important aspect of using reward systems. Engaging the individual in choice and discussion in relation to rewards is not only good practice but is also more likely to create a successful system. The degree to which this can be effective depends on the skills and understanding of the individual concerned but offering choice should be considered on every occasion.

Examples of visual reward systems

Visual reward systems can be used to show a child what the reward will be for completing the task or conforming to expectations, as in Figure 5.2.

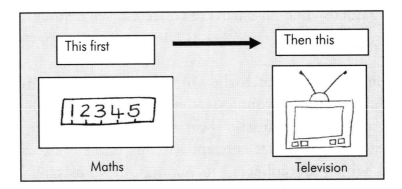

Figure 5.2 This first – then this

Using this type of visual representation gives a clear visual reminder of what will follow once a particular activity is completed. If this is done using a blank master card with Velcro slots for the activities, it can be used time and time again. A more complex type of this system is set out in Figure 5.3.

A more abstract representation, this sets out the number of things to do before 'big' reward. If needed, particularly whilst establishing the system, each smiley face can be exchanged for a small reward (e.g. a

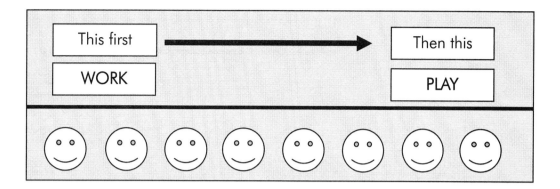

Figure 5.3 This first – then this 2

raisin, a few seconds with a sensory toy, etc.). The next system (Figure 5.4) shows the reward to come (a photo or symbol placed at the top) and breaks down tasks/expectations into steps. These steps can be photos of the stages of the task or can be single tasks to complete during one 'work' session.

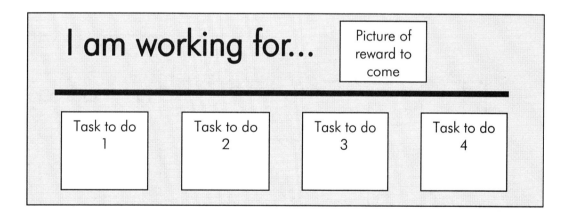

Figure 5.4 I am working for…

Another way of representing the same concept is set out in Figure 5.5. In this case, the steps are not represented visually but a token (a star) is given for each step or activity required to get to the final reward. The stars can represent stages/steps in a task or specific behaviours, for example concentrating for units of time, number of sums/lines, on-task behaviour, putting up hand, etc.

Figure 5.5 To Do chart

This next representation (Figure 5.6) shows a more meaningful system. Here, a picture of a train is cut into pieces, each piece stuck on the card with Velcro. One piece of the train is earned for each activity/task/ behaviour and stuck on the picture on the other side of the card. When the complete picture is made up, the reward is achieved.

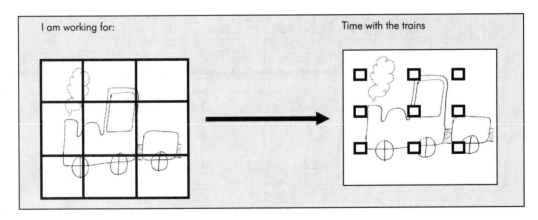

Figure 5.6 I am working for time with the trains

The use of a visual timetable or schedule can also be combined with a reward system using a schedule star or tick chart. This can be used with an individual who is used to working with a schedule system. The schedule chart can be used as a means of recording progress through the schedule or can be used in a more complex way to record the number of ticks or stars earned on a daily or even weekly basis. An example of a schedule chart is shown in Figure 5.7.

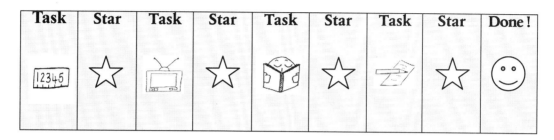

I have earned   STARS!

Figure 5.7 Star schedule

Star charts and variations

The use of star charts or sticker/token charts is very popular both with children and with schools and families. The individual simply collects stars or stickers and places them on the chart. When the chart is filled the reward is earned. This provides a visual representation of achievement and a means of self-monitoring progress towards the reward. This is a way of moving towards less concrete reward systems and can also be used to extend the reward period – it can take a whole day or week to fill in a star chart. It does however use an abstract model and relies on the individual understanding the way this system works. For this reason, this type of reward chart is best used only with those children and young people with ASD who have the level of understanding needed for this to be a successful reward tool. There are lots of examples of simple star charts which can be found on the web. Some popular examples are shown in Figures 5.8 to 5.13.

For individuals who are able to contribute to target setting and can manage the concept of working towards achieving multiple goals, a recording chart such as Table 5.13 can be used.

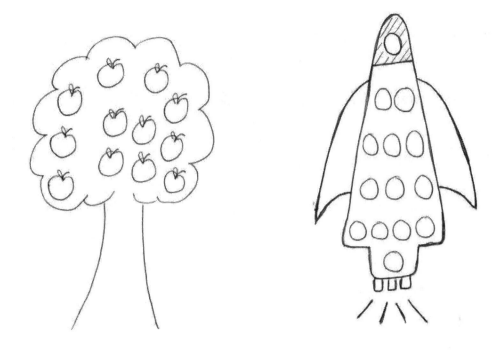

Figure 5.8 Collecting apples on the tree   Figure 5.9 Filling a rocket to the moon

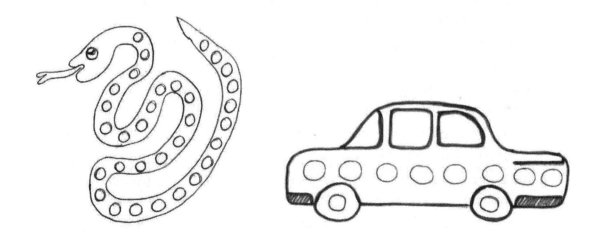

Figure 5.10 Completing a car and a snake

Figure 5.11 Putting wheels on a train   Figure 5.12 Colouring petals on a flower

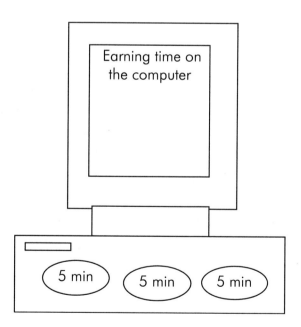

Figure 5.13 Earning time on the computer

Table 5.13 Example recording chart – 'I can do this!'

My aims	How am I doing?						
To tidy my room							
To finish my maths							
To play football with my friends							
To stay in assembly for the whole session							

Tokens or vouchers

For those individuals who have the level of understanding of abstract concepts needed, vouchers can be given as rewards to be collected and 'cashed in' at the end of the day for specified and pre-agreed items, or tokens can be given to be 'spent' at the end of a session or day in a reward 'shop'. Two examples of paper tokens are shown in Figure 5.14.

Concrete objects such as bricks in a tube or marbles in a jar can also be used as tokens and provide both a visual and physical means of providing reinforcement.

Removing rewards

Rewards earned for specific behaviour should not be removed once earned. Not doing what is required to earn the reward means that the reward is not achieved and this is a consequence in itself. If, whilst the

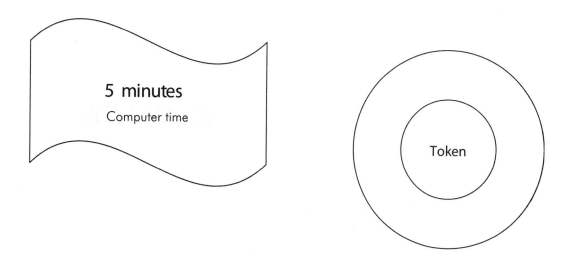

Figure 5.14 Tokens

individual is earning a reward for one behaviour, another undesirable behaviour occurs, this should be dealt with using the 'Red' strategies already identified. In most cases the use of a Red strategy would mean that there is a delay in achieving the reward aimed for (another natural consequence) and, once the Red strategy is applied and calm has emerged, the individual can move on to continue the earning of rewards (back to Green).

Recording reward systems

Details of any reward system used can be recorded (depending on the complexity of the system) on the Intervention Framework Flowchart or the Intervention Hierarchy sheet within the Green level or on the Teaching New Skills Record. If a more complex reward system is planned which cannot be accurately recorded on these sheets, the detail can be recorded on a separate 5P Reward Record sheet (See Table 5.14).

The record sheet requires that the behaviour identified for reward is precisely defined, that is making the required behaviour explicit and concrete. A number of prompt questions are given to aid the planning process:

Table 5.14 The 5P reward record

Name of child:　　　　　Reward agreed by:　　　　　Date of review:

Behaviour identified for reward/reinforcement (precisely defined):

Is this a new skill? If so, how will this be taught/encouraged?					
How will we know when this has happened? What will we see?					
Skill? Behaviour? Details:					
Prompts allowed? Details:					
Organization of reward system:					
1. Type of reward? (activity/sticker/token/toy/food, etc.)					
2. Frequency (each time? in stages?) Details:					
3. Duration (session/half day, full day, etc.) Details:					
4. Record for child (chart/box/tokens, etc.) Attach example					
5. Has child been involved in discussion/design of programme? Details:					
6. Record for staff/parent? Details: Attach example					

- Is this a new skill? If so, how will this be taught or encouraged?

- How will we know when this has happened? What will we see?

The organization of the reward system is also recorded including prompts allowed, type of reward (activity/sticker/token/toy/food, etc.), the frequency of the reward (each time? in stages?) and the duration (session, half day, full day, etc.). The record sheet also prompts good practice by asking for an example of the record used by the child or young person (i.e. a chart/box/tokens, etc.) and asking if the child or young person has been involved in discussion or design of the programme and whether a copy of the record has been shared with other staff or the parent.

A blank photocopiable copy of the 5P Reward Record sheet is set out in Table 5.14.

CHAPTER 6

Staying Green – Additional Practical Strategies for Behaviour Intervention

This chapter includes additional material which can be for everyday use (within the foundations) or used as part of a specific intervention programme. Building on the traffic light system introduced in the 5P Approach, the chapter has guidance on using the 5P traffic light system with individuals and class groups and using the 5P Approach to support children and young people to manage their feelings. Following this there are also some hints and tips on dealing with attention-seeking behaviour, managing avoidance behaviour, and giving directions.

Using the 5P traffic lights with individuals and class groups

'Traffic lights' are an easy way to visually show the three different levels of behaviour or stages in behaviour management and can be used with children and young people to support their understanding of the processes and to help them begin to recognize and manage (self-regulate) their own behaviour at each level. There are many examples to be found in schools of using this type of colour coding system. This section contains some additional ideas on how traffic lights can be used, as in other areas of the 5P Approach, with an emphasis on promoting prevention, involving the individual in the decision-making process and encouraging independence.

My Traffic Lights

The 'My Traffic Lights' sheet (p.94) can be used with the child or young person in one of two ways depending on the age and maturity of the individual concerned. The 5P 'My Traffic Lights' sheet can be used as a discussion tool to involve the child or young person in identifying which behaviours happen at each level and in decision making or problem solving about what should happen at each stage. These are then used to inform the decisions on the Intervention Hierarchy and also recorded on the sheet and used in the intervention programme. These materials can also be used to inform the child or young person about the programme by providing the individual with a visual representation of what will happen in the Intervention Framework (recorded by referring to the Intervention Hierarchy). The sheet can be given to the child or young person as a reminder of the stages or laminated and displayed on the wall (as appropriate).

A blank coloured copy of the My Traffic Lights sheet can be found at the end of the 5P Approach Intervention Framework Record (p.94).

Traffic Light Signals

Once the Intervention Framework has been completed and the adults working with the child or young person are clear which behaviours and strategies are linked to each colour, single traffic light colours can be used to signal which level the child or young person is currently at. Single traffic lights (on laminated card) are held up as a signal:

Green signals 'Good! Keep going, you are moving towards the reward'.

Amber signals 'Take a break, calm, stop and think' (to complete this refer to the Intervention Hierarchy for details of Amber strategies) and then there is a move back to Green behaviour ('you don't want to move to Red!').

Red signals 'Too late!' Agreed Red action (e.g. Time Out).

The specific behaviour or agreed strategy for each level can be written on the appropriate card.

Note: The purpose of using the three traffic light colours is to empower the child to recognize his or her own levels of behaviour and eventually learn to self-manage (that is to stay at Green or Amber). If adults or carers are using the traffic lights to signal to the child or young person which stage they are on, it is important that this does not become a negative routine used to signal warnings only. The Amber signal, although in a way serving as a warning, should be used to signal that it is time for an alternate behaviour (calm, stop and think, take a break, etc.) so that Green can be reached quickly. Once the Amber behaviour or action has occurred, the individual is quickly brought back to Green.

The language adults use at this stage is very important, as there is a need to avoid instructions sounding like a threat of punishment. For example, 'You are at Amber – it is time to stop and think – let's take a break' gives the right message, whereas 'You are at Amber, if you don't stop it is Time Out!' does not. In this way, the use of traffic lights in the 5P Approach differs from their use in other behaviour management books where an amber card may be used simply as a warning or threat of a punishment to come if the behaviour does not stop. In the 5P Approach, the Amber card signals or triggers a *behaviour* you expect the individual to follow, thus giving the individual something to do – a concrete and practical strategy for behaviour self-management. The use of Amber strategies aims all the time to empower the individual to recognize where they are in the behaviour cycle and provide strategies for them to avoid moving into the Red zone and instead move back to Green. Only in *extreme* cases (i.e. where no other strategies have worked) should the child or young person be given a limit to the number of times they can reach Amber before going to Red. Again this is where the 5P Approach differs from other uses of amber and red cards for behaviour management, some of which mirror the football match rule of two yellow cards and off the pitch! Red strategies or consequences are reserved for agreed Red behaviour and should not be used because the child or young person has had too many goes at Amber! (If this becomes a problem, and the child or young person always reaches Red, it is time to look again at the Intervention Hierarchy. There may be a need to review which behaviours are considered to be Red and to review the strategies being used.)

A blank coloured copy of the Traffic Light Signals can be found at the end of the 5P Approach Intervention Framework Record (p.95).

The 'Where am I now?' board

One variation on the use of coloured cards is to give the child or young person the card to hold as a signal/reminder *or* to place the card on the desk *or* to place the card on a 'Where am I now?' board (see Figure 6.1). The 'Where am I now?' board is a laminated card with a Velcro strip. A coloured card is placed on the board to signal to the child or young person which colour their current behaviour represents (i.e. Red, Amber or Green). At the base of the card is a written or pictorial reminder of the strategies which are linked with each colour.

Name (or photo):

Where am I now?

Velcro strip

<u>Reminder</u>
Green =
Amber =
Red =

Figure 6.1 Where am I now?

The indicator board

This can be used with individuals or with class groups to indicate how the child or children are doing at any given time. The photo of the child or young person can be moved from stage to stage to give a visual indicator of where they are (see Figure 6.2).

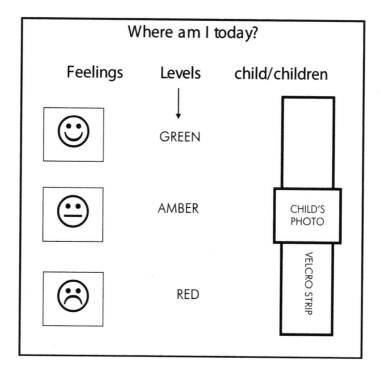

Figure 6.2 Indicator board

This type of chart can be made using varying levels of complexity (written names, written strategies within the colours, etc.) according to the age and level of maturity of the child or children concerned.

Again, this chart is used as a visual representation to aid the child or young person to recognize and manage their behaviour. It should be used in conjunction with a system of rewards or reinforcing activities and *not* used as a threat of punishment or loss of reward to come!

Using the 5P Traffic Light system to help children and young people to manage their feelings and behaviour

The 5P Intervention Hierarchy, used to set out strategies for behaviour intervention, can also be used in an adapted form to give a visual reminder to the child or young person of the strategies used to manage feelings. A blank coloured example can be found at the end of the 5P Approach Intervention Framework Record (p.97).

As with behaviour intervention, the three traffic light colours are used to represent differing stages in the management of emotions and to set out clear strategies which can be used at the three different levels, with the purpose of promoting independence in managing emotions such as anger and anxiety. Once the adult has worked out what the behaviour signals are at each level, they can discuss with the child or young person (if appropriate) what the signals might look like (and feel like) when they are becoming angry/anxious, etc. and what strategies they might adopt. This type of system can be used successfully with programmes such as 'How does your engine run' used by many occupational therapists (see, for example, Williams and Shellenberger 1996) to support children and young people in recognizing the physical responses and feelings in their body at different levels of arousal.

Another strategy would be to use a wall chart to indicate what stage the child or young person is at in managing their feelings. A coloured, photocopiable example is found at the end of the Intervention Framework Record (p.97). As with the indicator board (Figure 6.2), a name card or photograph of the child can be placed at the appropriate level on the Velcro strip.

Relaxation stories

The following story can be used as a role play exercise coupled with discussion and the use of coloured pens to indicate the stage of anxiety or anger. Used with relaxation techniques and practical examples of how to relax, recognize and manage feelings practically, this makes a good personal 'story' for the child or young person to relate to and refer to as an aide-memoire.

The story is about a tortoise (the child can give it a name) who starts by feeling happy and relaxed (Green) and then as the story progresses becomes worried (Amber), then very worried (Red), and finally goes into his shell to hide from the worry. Inside the shell the tortoise relaxes (Amber) and begins to slowly and gradually come out of the shell and back to continue the walk (Green).

The story can be personalized to cover specific circumstances then used as a permanent record (perhaps in the form of a laminated book or strip) of the strategies the child will use if he or she feels worried or angry, rather like the use of a Social Story (developed by Carol Gray).

Photocopiable templates which can be used and coloured as needed for this story are set on the following pages (Figure 6.3).

My Turtle Story

My Turtle's name is:

I'm happy

I'm happy

Oh dear!

What colour?

Figure 6.3 My Turtle Story

Figure 6.3 My Turtle Story cont.

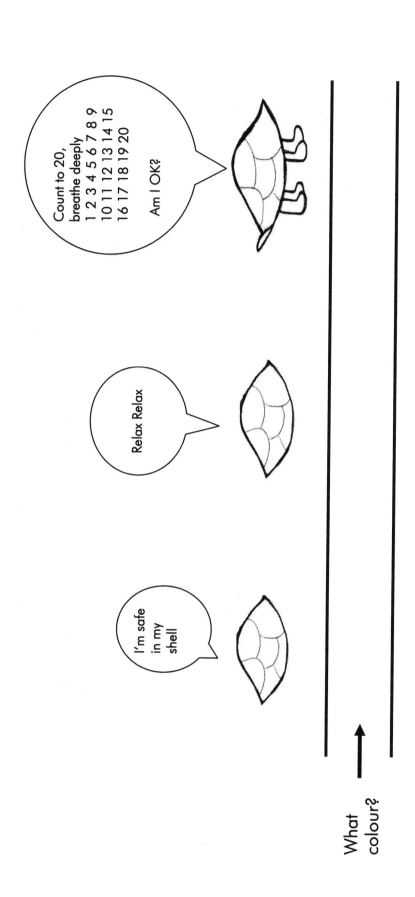

Figure 6.3 My Turtle Story cont.

Figure 6.3 My Turtle Story cont.

Encouraging self-management

This system, based on the comic strip approach developed by Carol Gray (1994), also uses the traffic light system to promote the management and recognition of feelings and emotions. As in the 'Tortoise Story', coloured pens are used to represent feelings – Green (I'm OK), Amber (getting worried/bubbling), Red (danger!). As the child moves through the 'story' a coloured pathway is drawn according to the level of anxiety/anger at each stage. It is also important to help the individual to recognize the behaviours or feelings which accompany the emotions by representing these in a concrete way with the use of pictures (provided or self-drawn) to serve as a visual reminder and also to support understanding. Again, as with the tortoise story, the aim would be to illustrate the whole cycle from Green through Amber and Red and back to Green. This can be represented visually in a strip as in Figure 6.4 or in a circle.

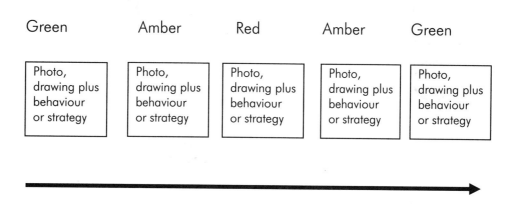

Figure 6.4 Traffic Light cycle

Which route to take?

For those individuals who are able to understand the more complex concepts of choice, Red, Amber and Green colours and pictures can also be used to map out good and bad choices or routes (see Figure 6.5). This gives the individual a visual representation of the consequences of taking certain routes, helps to serve as a reminder of the

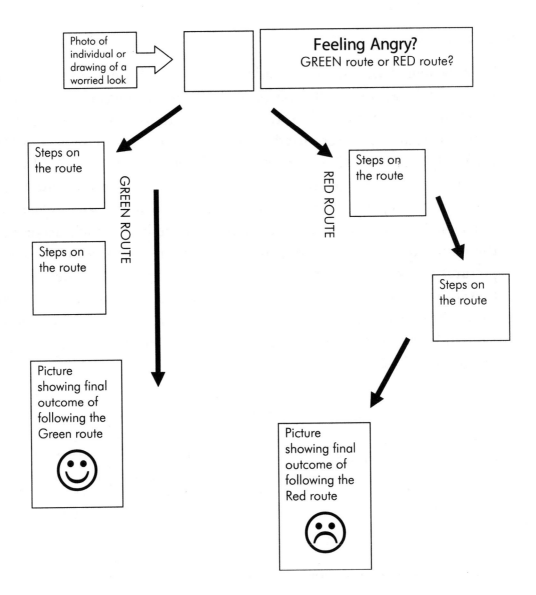

Figure 6.5 Routes

behaviours concerned and can be used by adults at the Amber stage to represent the situation to the individual and promote independence by providing supported choice. The best use of this type of tool is for the child or young person to fully participate in setting out the choices and consequences, making use of the colours to denote the stage and even drawing the pictures needed themselves.

Attention-seeking behaviour

Question: What is attention-seeking behaviour? Answer: Behaviour which occurs with the sole purpose of seeking someone's attention.

When we describe behaviour as attention seeking we often see this as the cause or function of a behaviour we feel is inappropriate and thus adopt a general strategy of ignoring (or not rewarding) the behaviour. However, before deciding upon a strategy for dealing with what we see as attention-seeking behaviour, we need to look more closely at the root cause of the attention-seeking. Attention-seeking behaviour always has a function. This may be:

- to initiate or sustain interaction with someone

- to avoid something or someone

- to divert from something or to something

- to communicate in some way (e.g. to ask for help, a break, to show dislike, to express an emotion, etc.).

Whichever function it is serving, attention-seeking behaviour indicates that the child or young person does not have (or perhaps does not want to use) an appropriate strategy to gain the attention. The first step in dealing with what we consider to be attention-seeking behaviour is therefore to work out the function of the behaviour. The stages of the 5P Approach can help with this. Once the function has been identified, a strategy can be used which addresses the issue. If we apply a blanket strategy of avoiding attention-seeking behaviour this might well serve to escalate rather than extinguish the behaviour. For example, if a child or young person is trying to gain attention (whether inappropriately or not) to communicate pain or thirst, ignoring this will not make the behaviour go away but simply make the situation worse. The assumption that if ignored the child or young person may adopt a more appropriate means of gaining attention relies on the individual having both the skills to do so and a sufficient understanding of people (a difficulty for those with ASD) to read the situation and recognize an alternative means of communicating. Having ascertained the function, some strategies which may be useful for differing circumstances include the following.

If the attention-seeking behaviour is intended to initiate interaction:

1. Provide an alternate means of gaining attention (i.e. teach a skill).

2. Ignore or give minimal attention to inappropriate means of gaining attention (if you are sure that the individual knows an appropriate means! You may need a prompt!).

3. Reward appropriate behaviour when it occurs naturally, making it clear to the individual that this is a good way of initiating interaction.

If the attention-seeking is a way to avoid something, see the separate 'Managing avoidance behaviour' guidance later in the chapter.

If the attention-seeking behaviour is a means of communicating:

1. Using the 5P Approach, first revisit the 'foundations'.

2. Provide alternate means of communicating.

3. Provide coping strategies and teach new skills (if needed).

4. Reward use of the new communication strategy.

Remember Red, Amber and Green!

- Ignore Green behaviour (if identified as part of a strategy within the whole behaviour Intervention Framework).

- Divert or distract at Amber.

- Action/signal at Red.

Do not ignore behaviours which:

- always escalate – place these at Amber and use an Amber strategy

- are a danger to the child or others (these are always Red)

- are destructive (Red – see 'Why change behaviour?' in the 5P Prioritizing section).

If these Red behaviours occur and can't be ignored, use a Time Out strategy by using a 'cold, calm and quiet' approach to give minimal attention (by avoiding eye contact, giving minimal verbal interaction, etc.). Then:

1. wait for a 'calm' signal

2. re-focus or re-schedule to a new behaviour

3. reward appropriate behaviour.

Managing avoidance behaviour

This section provides some practical strategies which can be used with children and young people who may be avoiding direction or change, may be avoiding things because of sensory issues or fears or phobias, may be avoiding because of stimulatory or obsessive interests or who may be avoiding eating.

Strategies for those who are avoiding direction

- Use visual representation of directions or instructions such as written or pictorial lists of rules, use of schedules, mini-schedules or visual 'jigs'. The strategy would be to re-state the rule or re-schedule (by pointing to the schedule or directing to the schedule board) and then reward the individual for following the direction.

- Use 'pulling not pushing' methods such as a 'This first – then this' card or a 'I am working for...' card (see Chapter 5). This can be done using objects, photos, pictures or written text as appropriate to the individual. Then follow with a motivating activity.

Strategies for those who are avoiding change

- Pre-empt or give an advance warning of things to come. Use a countdown system (3:2:1), make use of a timer or pinger as a signal or a song or music cue. For example, use a musical/song cue for tidying the room at transition time and then couple this with a Social Story or photos of what is to come next.

- Plan change and build in surprise! Add a surprise symbol to the child or young person's schedule or use this as as a direction card. It is important to begin with a pleasant or rewarding surprise ('it's biscuits or bike time') and when the individual is able to cope successfully with this type of change, move on to other less rewarding or pleasant changes. Do this by starting with a very short changed activity followed by the expected activity or rewarding activity (e.g. when expecting playtime give a surprise of two minutes singing and then follow the usual routine to go out to play).

- Use a transition object/activity. Allow the individual to take a favoured toy or activity to support change and to distract or reduce anxiety. This can also be done by placing a photo or symbol of the place/activity next in the timetable.

- Use 'This first – then…'. This has already been mentioned within this book and has many uses. Used in this instance it relates to issues with change and transition.

Strategies for those avoiding due to fears, phobias or sensory issues

Adopt a general approach of planning changes in small steps or chains and adding one step at a time, or teach separate steps and join when all steps are learned. This can then be followed by altering distance (i.e. bringing the avoided item closer), altering time (making the time near the item longer) and moving from pretend to real.

For example, if a child or young person is afraid of entering the noisy classroom you can devise a chain of steps to overcome the fear, by the child following footsteps on the floor into the classroom then to a chair, then sitting on the chair, then completing a task and then going out to play. These are gradually extended with success and the length of time and level of prompting reduced until the task is achieved independently.

Sensory issues can be addressed by establishing confidence and familiarity with the avoided sensory experience (e.g. noise, textures, etc.) in short play situations. Gradually increase the length of time and range of sensory experiences and extend to real situations when the child is comfortable within the play situation. Make use of pre-empting and warning and also Social Stories (written or pictorial) to prepare the child for a sensory experience they may dislike (e.g. fire bell). Make alterations to the environment if practically possible whilst establishing behaviour change (e.g. use of headphones). It is also useful to revisit the 5P Foundations.

Strategies for those avoiding eating

It is important to note that eating problems may also relate to sensory issues and should be addressed with this in mind (see above).

General eating-related strategies include:

- Use a schedule or food choice board (see 'Giving directions' below).

- Take the pressure off by implementing the smallest possible change at a time.

- Vary food texture, shape, colour, taste (one at a time in *very* small steps).

- Give a little non-preferred food with a lot of preferred food.

- Practise familiarizing with different food textures, tastes and smells at non-meal times.

- Establish a set dinner routine and represent this visually – show a menu (with choices if appropriate), give a pictorial or written list of the mealtime process and end with a 'finished' symbol.

- Avoid between meal eating by using a reminder card by the fridge or table – 'the next meal is at…, if you are still hungry ask for fruit' (this can be done using a fruit request card if needed).

- Make a choice list – Red (not eaten) foods and Green (preferred) foods and use a visually presented 'This first (Red food, very small amount) – then choice of… (Green foods)' card.

- Provide labelled snacks and meals to prevent sibling issues.

Strategies for those avoiding due to stimulatory issues and obsessions

Again, it is important to note that these problems may also relate to sensory issues and should be addressed with this in mind (see above). The technique to use here is ration – restrict – change or shape behaviour. The aim would be to shift the balance of time spent on these activities rather than totally remove them. The child or young person should of course have the opportunity to spend time on their preferred activities but this should not get to the degree that it causes problems (see 'Why change behaviour?' in the 5P Prioritizing section in Chapter 3) and should not be allowed to continue when the situation is inappropriate and may cause social issues which make the child or young person vulnerable (e.g. humming loudly in the cinema, stroking someone's soft jumper). Changing this type of behaviour can be done by making use of the following strategies:

- This first – then…

- Not this – do this (offering a functionally equivalent alternative behaviour).

- Using a schedule.

- Using Social Stories.

Giving directions using visual cues

In addition to avoiding difficulties that children and young people with ASD may have in understanding others' verbally presented instructions, the use of visual materials to give direction also serves to decrease stress levels and gives a clear signal to show what is required. The use of visual materials also avoids confrontation which might occur at times of stress or misunderstanding. The following examples use pictures or diagrams to give direction.

The 'This first – then this' card examples given in Chapter 5 (Figures 5.2 and 5.3) give a visual representation of what will follow once a particular activity is completed. This next card 'Not this – do this' (Figure 6.6) gives a clear message showing that current behaviour is not acceptable and also shows what should be happening. If these cards are laminated with Velcro attachments, symbols can be changed to suit the particular circumstances.

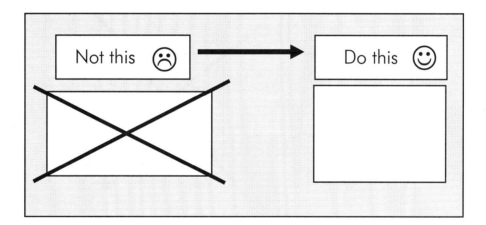

Figure 6.6 Not this – do this

Visual reward systems (see 'Rewards, motivators and reinforcers' in Chapter 5 for examples) can be used to show a child what the reward will be for completing the task or conforming to expectations. Another example is given in Figure 6.7. Completed tasks from the 'I am working for' board can be taken from the board to give a visual picture of progress towards the goal.

Single pictures (see Figure 6.8) can be used to give directions (e.g. quiet, stop, sit down, etc.). Crosses can be used to denote 'no...' (e.g. no talking, no pinching).

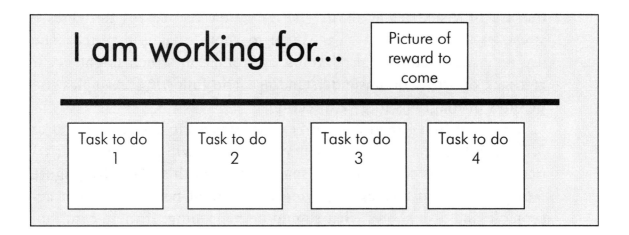

Figure 6.7 I am working for... 2

Figure 6.8 Single pictures for direction

Many schools now use a 'swatch' or key ring system to aid communication of key information. Copies of regularly used symbols (e.g. toilet, quiet, stop, listen) are kept together on a key ring attached to a belt. In this way symbols are easily accessible to both adult and child/young person at all times, wherever you are!

It is important to remember however that any photos, pictures or symbols used must be appropriate to the child/young person's age and level of ability and used consistently across all environments (school using one type of symbol and home using another is very confusing!).

Schedules or timetables

These can be used effectively to give direction and provide a clear outline of what is expected within the specified timescale. Schedules can be used equally well to show behaviour or learning routines. Some examples of how schedules can be used in this way follow.

Visual timetables are used commonly in schools and in the home. Used within the TEACCH approach and within PECS, they can be displayed from top to bottom or side to side. Children can remove the symbols as each activity is completed and place them within a 'finished' envelope or box (Figure 6.9). This gives a visual view of progress. Visual timetables not only provide a visual representation giving direction to the child or young person but can also provide an overview of the day/session with clear reference of what is to come. Using timetables and schedules therefore helps to provide a safe and predictable environment.

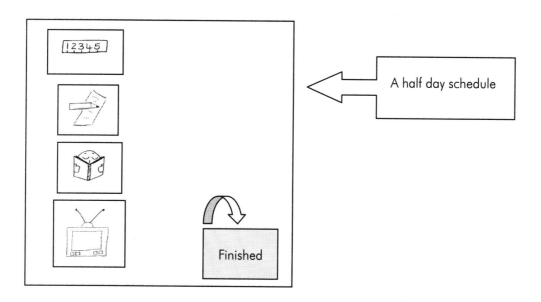

Figure 6.9 Half day schedule

In the example in Figure 6.10, the child or young person can tick or cross out activities as they progress through them. This can also be linked to a reward system and encourages self-monitoring of on-task behaviour. This type of timetable can easily be recorded on a whiteboard.

The schedule in Figure 6.11 is similar to a daily schedule but is used for individual activities or tasks (sometimes known as a visual jig). The child progresses through the steps in turn until the task is completed. This task breakdown can be presented in written or pictorial form and can also be linked to reward systems. This type of approach is useful for those children and young people who have organizational problems, as it encourages on-task behaviour and independence.

My Daily Schedule

9.00 – 10.00	literacy	
10.00 – 10.45	numeracy	
10.45 – 11.00	break	
11.00 – 12.00	music	
12.00 – 1.00	lunch	
1.00 – 2.00	PE	
2.00 – 3.00	science	
3.45	Home !!	

A schedule in written form with room to tick tasks completed

Figure 6.10 My daily schedule

Mini schedule: task

1	Press the switch to turn on the computer	
2	Wait until the pictures load	
3	Use the mouse to point to the game you want	
4	Click once on the left button	
5	Wait until the pictures load	
6	Type your name in the box	
7	Press return	
8	Start to play!	

A breakdown of steps in a task

Figure 6.11 Mini schedule: task

Similar to above, behaviour routines can be broken down into stages or steps (see Figure 6.12). Again this can be linked to a reward system if appropriate.

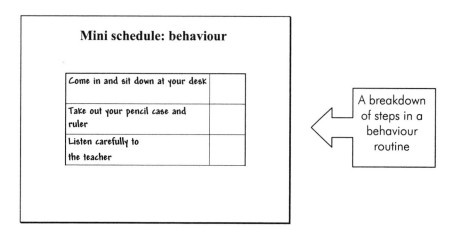

Figure 6.12 Mini schedule: behaviour

CHAPTER 7

Where Next?

By now you should be familiar with the overall structure of the 5P Approach. To give you some idea of how it can be put into practice, there now follow four case studies which demonstrate how the system is put to practical use. Each one throws up a very different set of problems and the children concerned are of very different ages and abilities. But the case studies demonstrate the way in which the 5P Approach Intervention Framework as outlined in this book can be easily adapted to meet widely differing situations. Each case study follows the common pattern of the 5P Approach Intervention Framework, using the five stages as its guide. Each one begins with an outline of the situation.

The conclusions and planning for each case study are my own and are based on my own hypotheses. These case studies can however also be used to practise the use of the 5P Approach Intervention Framework, in training or for group discussion. The basic information can be recorded on the 5P Approach Intervention Recording sheets for quick reference and new strategies developed from your own problem-solving and planning discussions.

Case study one – Robin

Situation

Robin is seven years old and attends a local mainstream primary school. She has a diagnosis of high functioning autism. Her teachers are becoming increasingly concerned about her behaviour. She is reported to be an able child and popular with her peers but there are daily temper tantrums which frequently result in her being removed from class and sometimes her mother is called to take her home to give her a chance to calm down.

Profile information

(to be recorded on the 5P Profile)

1. LIKES AND INTERESTS

Books and shop catalogues. Listening to taped stories. The colour purple. Drawing and colouring. Teddies and soft toys.

2. DISLIKES, FEARS AND WORRIES

Dislikes parties and crowded places. Frightened of fire alarms, motorbikes and hand dryers in toilets.

3. COMMUNICATION

Expressive language and comprehension skills assessed as being within the average to above average range. Some difficulties with abstract concepts and verbal reasoning and some difficulties with keeping to the topic of conversation. Difficulties in talking about herself and her feelings.

4. LEARNING/COGNITIVE STYLE, STRENGTHS AND PREFERENCES

Average to above average ability in all areas but some difficulties with problem solving particularly where there is no visual or practical support. A visual learner.

5. DIFFICULTIES AND WEAKNESSES

Some problems with both personal organization and organization within her learning. Problems with 'thinking, planning and doing' particularly within social situations, often panics and doesn't know what to do in difficult situations.

6. SENSORY ISSUES

Sensory profile shows sensitivity to noise and busy environments. Hypersensitive to temperature. Dislikes spicy or strongly flavoured food. Likes soft textures.

Prioritizing

Only one major problem – temper tantrums.

Problem Analysis

(to be recorded on the Problem Solving Summary sheet)

A BBB C chart and informal observation used. Robin's behaviour seems to have a pattern. The first sign that things are not right is that Robin begins to hum to herself and may put her hands over her ears. The humming becomes louder and she begins to rock on her seat. The last stage is when she rocks on her seat more violently, sometimes pushing over the table and getting up, making very loud noises and crying, often throwing herself to the floor. Observation indicates that attempts to talk to her when she begins to hum makes her hum louder and seems to make things worse. If she becomes really distressed, touching her or taking her by the hand often provokes an aggressive outburst where she may push or hit out. Once at the tantrum stage she takes a while to calm down, particularly if the adult talks to her or touches her. If she can find her soft toy this seems to act as a comforter.

No particular trigger was identified but these events seemed to happen in unstructured lessons, in the hall or dining room or when the room was particularly stuffy or hot.

Problem Solving

(to be recorded on the Problem Solving Summary sheet)

The hypothesis was that Robin's problems in school had a sensory base. Disliking busy and noisy environments, if the class becomes noisy she becomes increasingly uncomfortable. She tries to blot out noise and take control by humming and covering her ears but if the noise continues her behaviour deteriorates. She has no means of indicating (or perhaps recognizing) that she is becoming stressed and does not ask for help.

Plan

(to be recorded on the Planning Summary sheet and the Intervention Hierarchy sheet)

GREEN 1: FOUNDATIONS

Provision of a sensory diet. Careful consideration of the sensory environment, including placing Robin in a quiet part of the classroom. Provision of a distraction-free area for activities when the class may become noisy. Building in timed sensory breaks (listening to a tape, reading a catalogue) as part of her schedule. Use of earmuffs at noisy times if Robin feels happy with this.

GREEN 2: NEW SKILLS TO BE TAUGHT

Work with the OT on developing an awareness of the physical signs of stress/anxiety and calming techniques. Use of a visual scale to show how she is feeling. Learning to request a break when feeling stressed. Learning a relaxation routine prompted by visual schedule.

GREEN 2: REWARDS OR REINFORCING ACTIVITIES

Sensory breaks using catalogues, taped stories and drawing.

AMBER STRATEGIES

At first signs, adult offers earmuffs or time working in the distraction-free area. If this doesn't work or is refused, adult prompts to take a sensory break (using a break card to request, timed). Adult supports Robin to take a break. Over time, decrease prompting to encourage Robin to use strategies independently.

RED STRATEGIES

Instruction to move to the Red zone (a bean bag with a soft blanket and soft toy) using a photo card rather than voice. Physical prompt to the Red zone if needed, using minimal touch. As soon as Robin shows signs of calming, prompt with visual mini schedule to follow a relax routine. Once calm, reward verbally with 'well done, you are calm, do you need a break?' Offer drawing or story tape (this first – then work) as a bridge to returning to class. (Note: reward follows calm behaviour *not* tantrum).

Case study two – Jake

Situation

Jake is six. He has a diagnosis of severe autism and attends the local special school which caters for children with learning difficulty including those on the autistic spectrum. Jake is described by both school and home as being very 'changeable'. At times he can be calm and happy and at others aggressive towards adults. A particular concern at school is pinching as this can sometimes draw blood.

Profile information

1. LIKES AND INTERESTS

Cars and trains and anything that works mechanically. Taking things apart. Playing on his own.

2. DISLIKES, FEARS AND WORRIES

Other children. Adults too close (unless of his choosing). Doesn't like being directed. Dislikes change of routine.

3. COMMUNICATION

Described as non-verbal. Some limited use of key signs (toilet, drink, etc.). Some limited use of PECS (Stage One).

4. LEARNING/COGNITIVE STYLE, STRENGTHS AND PREFERENCES

Prefers to do his own thing. Good at puzzles and construction. Knows his numbers and letters (can match and point to on request). Dislikes being rushed or finishing halfway through something.

5. DIFFICULTIES AND WEAKNESSES

Refuses to do drawing, writing or any pencil work. Poor understanding of spoken language. Difficulty with social play and social interaction with peers or adults (little interest).

6. SENSORY ISSUES

Profiling indicates a pattern of both sensory-seeking and sensory-avoidance behaviour according to the sense. He seeks tactile experiences on his own terms but dislikes firm touch. He smells and licks toys, people, etc. to explore. He avoids loud and sudden noises. He likes watching things that spin or shine.

Prioritizing

Behaviours identified for change:

- following direction
- taking things apart
- spinning or twirling things

- licking or smelling objects

- pinching.

Problem identified as priority – pinching.

Problem Analysis

The use of A BBB C chart and general observation followed by frequency counts showed different patterns and frequencies of pinching behaviour.

1. Light pinching or stroking behaviour (Jake seems almost unaware that he is doing this).

2. Frequent small pinches often accompanied by a whining noise. This seems to occur during group sessions.

3. Hard, sharp pinching which appears to follow a request to change activity or when a peer has intervened in his play.

Problem Solving

The hypothesis is that Jake's pinching is multifunctional:

1. as a sensory need

2. as a sign that he is becoming stressed

3. as a response to extreme upset.

Plan

GREEN 1: FOUNDATIONS

Provision of a sensory diet. Use of a visual schedule and visual markers. Sensory-based, practical and functional curriculum. Use of a total communication environment with emphasis on increasing his functional use of PECS within the classroom. Directions given using photos or symbols (staff use a symbol key ring). Careful planning of all transitions to ensure pre-warning of things to come, clear beginning and end points to activities, etc.

GREEN 2: NEW SKILLS TO BE TAUGHT

Increase spontaneous use of PECS. Tolerance of others alongside in play situations. Following one-step directions. Working within a group situation.

GREEN 2: REWARDS OR REINFORCING ACTIVITIES

Play-Doh, cornflour and water play. Tactile play box (materials, squidgy toys, etc.). Trains and car play. 'This first – then this' cards.

AMBER STRATEGIES

1. Soft pinching/stroking – gentle diversion to a small soft toy or piece of Blu-tack.

2. Frequent pinching (sign of stress) – diversion to a short break with tactile box (timed with a pinger or sand timer) and then back to situation with a 'This first – then this' card. Activity followed by preferred activity such as train play (timed).

RED STRATEGIES

Signal photo card 'No pinching'. Direction to 'hands down' (may need gentle physical prompt) – as soon as hands down achieved, wait two seconds and then use verbal praise (good – hands down) and photo-card direction to a sensory break (timed by pinger or sand timer and 'This first – then...' introduced to show what activity comes next). (Note: The reward (sensory break) follows hands down behaviour *not* Red pinching behaviour.)

Case study three – Evan

Situation

Evan is 15 and attends a local secondary school. He has a diagnosis of Asperger Syndrome. He is described by his teachers as verbally able and has a high word reading and spelling age. His teachers are increasingly concerned that he is falling behind academically and not completing his work in class. He frequently becomes noisy and sometimes verbally aggressive. His teachers feel he is showing signs of stress but if they offer help he shouts and walks out of class.

Profile information

1. LIKES AND INTERESTS

Animals. Computer games. Anything to do with the sea. 'CSI'.

2. DISLIKES, FEARS AND WORRIES

Feeling foolish. Failure.

3. COMMUNICATION

Very articulate with good expressive and receptive language skills. Verbal comprehension OK but sometimes needs time to assimilate longer and more complex verbal information.

4. LEARNING/COGNITIVE STYLE, STRENGTHS AND PREFERENCES

Very visual learner. Good at practical activities and tasks. Good at rule-based and mechanical tasks.

5. DIFFICULTIES AND WEAKNESSES

Difficulties with planning and organizing work. Difficulty processing information at speed. Poor problem-solving skills. Difficulty with abstracting information from text, inference and deduction.

6. SENSORY ISSUES

None noted.

Prioritizing

Priority 1 – shouting and walking out of class.
Priority 2 – completing work set.

Problem Analysis

Use of A BBB C and discussion with SENCo (Special Educational Needs Coordinator), class-based learning support and teachers indicated that Evan appeared to become aggressive and noisy in situations where he was required to give written answers or complete complex tasks independently. There was no particular trigger but a pattern which suggested the aggressive and difficult behaviour followed work-related problems. This would begin by him throwing down his pen and sighing. Difficult behaviour also increased when he was offered help.

Problem Solving

The hypothesis was that Evan was experiencing difficulty with aspects of school work which involved planning, organizing and sequencing or completing tasks at speed. This was raising anxiety and causing behaviour issues to emerge. His fear of failure and concern about feeling foolish was exacerbated when offered help which was making the situation worse for him.

Plan

GREEN 1: FOUNDATIONS

Teachers use of visual materials for planning, organizing and sequencing information (spider diagrams, flow charts, mind maps, etc.). Material presented in chunks and in a staged manner. System for asking for help put into place for whole class (using a visual traffic light signal).

Pre and post teaching by Learning Support Assistant (LSA) for tasks identified as being potentially difficult for him.

GREEN 2: NEW SKILLS TO BE TAUGHT

Work on self-image and self-esteem. Anxiety management and anger management and relaxation skills. Asking for help. Independently using visual strategies to plan, organize and sequence (spider diagrams, flow charts, mind maps, etc.).

GREEN 2: REWARDS OR REINFORCING ACTIVITIES

Weekly sessions helping the science teacher to clean the animals. A daily tick sheet for him to self-record success in 'keeping cool' and 'asking for help'. (In conjunction with parents) earning parts of a ticket to visit the London Zoo.

AMBER STRATEGIES

At first sign of throwing down pen, a quiet visual written reminder to ask for help or to ask for a short break (a cool down time). This can be time (specified length) outside class (supervised area if nearby) or within class reading a magazine (sea or animal related). Reminder of reward and record keeping and support to return to the task which had caused difficulty.

RED STRATEGIES

Immediate Time Out (two minutes timed with timer or clock) out of class in supervised area (staff dependent) or within class. Once calm, offer a short break and time for a re-think. Reminder of reward and record keeping and support to return to the task which had caused difficulty.

Case study four – Simon

Situation

Simon is 11. He has a diagnosis of high functioning autism. He has just transferred to a secondary school which has an integrated specialist provision for pupils with autistic spectrum disorder. After a few teething problems, Simon settled well into the secondary routines and is supported in most lessons by a learning support assistant. However he is experiencing increasing difficulty in class, particularly with his peers. Recently he has been put on report for shouting at pupils, pushing them out of the way and throwing things at them. No one knows what the reason is as Simon has previously always been friendly towards his peers.

Profile information

1. LIKES AND INTERESTS

Computer games. Cars and motorcycles. Reading. Chess.

2. DISLIKES, FEARS AND WORRIES

Dislikes crowded places such as supermarkets. Frightened of dogs. Worries that he will miss the bus home or forget his school books, PE kit, etc.

3. COMMUNICATION

Verbally very able. Answers well in class and uses sophisticated language and language structures.

4. LEARNING/COGNITIVE STYLE, STRENGTHS AND PREFERENCES

Very visual learner. Good with rule-based activities and mechanical maths. Likes all school work and a bit of a perfectionist (likes everything to be very neat and tidy).

5. DIFFICULTIES AND WEAKNESSES

Organizing his personal possessions (tends to overcompensate for this and worries he'll lose something). A bit clumsy and poor at sport. Finds it hard to stand in a line and to stand close to people. Has difficulties expressing his feelings and emotions.

6. SENSORY ISSUES

Picky eater, dislikes things with sauce or mushy foods. Sensitive to materials and certain clothes (cuts all labels out of shirts, etc.).

Prioritizing

Although there are some issue relating to peer interaction, organization skills and managing anxiety and worry, the priority has to be the current behaviour issues in class as these may cause a danger to others.

Problem Analysis

The A BBB C chart and discussion with the learning support assistant seems to show a pattern. Simon initially settles in class and joins in class discussions without incident. Issues begin to arise when the class is set to do individual work. Simon initially settles well but will soon start to mutter and name call to the person next to him ('go away stupid', 'don't touch my things'). This frequently escalates to him pushing at his peer's book or pushing at his peer. This further escalates into aggressive behaviour and throwing things. A second observation indicated that once Simon began to mutter to his peers and gently push things to one side, his peer would move Simon's books or pencil or remove his ruler or rubber in retaliation.

Problem Solving

The hypothesis is that Simon is experiencing difficulty in working alongside his peers and in ensuring his personal space. He feels peers encroach on his space and this causes anxiety and a behaviour reaction.

In turn, his peers aggravate the situation by touching his things and moving further into his space.

Plan

GREEN 1: FOUNDATIONS

Where possible sensitive placement within the classes – end of a row, space between Simon and the next peer. Use of a worry book and mentor to reduce anxiety. Sensory work on proprioceptive skills and tolerance of proximity of others. Work with whole peer group on ASD awareness including buddy system and circle of friends work.

GREEN 2: NEW SKILLS TO BE TAUGHT

Personal organization strategies. Relaxation and anger management strategies.

GREEN 2: REWARDS OR REINFORCING ACTIVITIES

Computer time (voucher system).

AMBER STRATEGIES

At signs of muttering, LSA intervenes and establishes the 'boundaries' of desk space (could mark with a strip or marker pen if needed) between Simon and his peer. Simon reminded to re-focus and record a worry in his worry book for later discussion.

Simon encouraged to gauge his level of stress (using a visual emotions strip and supported by LSA initially). If at the level of needing a short break, Simon encouraged to take an 'exit' card and take a five minute break out of class. Computer voucher given for returning to class and resuming work.

RED STRATEGIES

If Red stage reached, Simon told clearly to 'Stop' and to exit the class (exit card shown) to go to a pre-agreed place nearby (accompanied by LSA). Simon asked to sit quietly for a minute and, when calm, to read through a Social Story which explains what happens and what to do. Return to class but sit with space. Rewarded for returning and regaining control by use of computer at break time (voucher given).

And finally…

By now you should have a good working knowledge of the 5P Approach, so all that remains is to put it into practice! At all times you should try to keep in mind the process of the 5Ps:

Profile – make sure you know the child or young person well.

Prioritize – decide which behaviour you are going to start with.

Problem Analysis – get as much clear information as you can about what *exactly* is happening.

Problem Solve – use all the information you have to form a hypothesis about *why* the behaviour or situation is arising.

Plan – draw up a comprehensive intervention plan that goes further than just 'what to do when x does this' and sets out staged strategies in the traffic light colours, identifies skills to teach and learn, and the rewards to use.

The 5P Approach, with its solution-focused emphasis, sets out to ensure that any strategies developed and used in the process quickly become part of the general approach (the autism-friendly environment) and become established as part of the foundations (going back to Green!). When a problem occurs, using the 5P Approach takes you through a clear pathway from Red (the most difficult behaviour) back to Green as soon as possible. This move through traffic light colours and back to Green is a core theme of the 5P Approach.

GOOD LUCK!

References

Baron-Cohen, S., Leslie, A.M. and Frith, U. (1985) 'Does the autistic child have a "Theory of Mind"?' *Cognition 21*, 1, 37–46.

Department for Education and Skills (2002) *Autistic Spectrum Disorders, Good Practice Guidance*. London: DfES.

Frith, U. (1989) *Autism: Explaining the Enigma*. Oxford: Blackwell.

Frost, L. and Bondy, A. (1994) *PECS Training Manual*. Brighton: Pyramid Educational Consultant.

Gray, C. (1994) *Comic Strip Conversations*. Jenison, MI: Jenison Public Schools.

Jordan, R. and Powell, S. (1995) *Understanding and Teaching Children with Autism*. Chichester: Wiley.

National Initiative for Autism: Screening and Assessment (NIASA) (2002) *National Autism Plan for Children (NAP-C)*. London: The National Autistic Society.

Powell, S. and Jordan, R. (1997) *Autism and Learning – A Guide to Good Practice*. London: David Fulton Publishers.

Williams, M.S. and Shellenberger, S. (1996) *How Does Your Engine Run? A Leader's Guide to the Alert Program for Self-Regulation*. Albuquerque, NM: Therapy Works.

Wing, L. and Gould, J. (1979) 'Severe impairments of social interaction and associated abnormalities in children: epidemiology and classification.' *Journal of Autism and Developmental Disorders 9*, 1, 11–29.

Index